You should Write that Down

Stories Along the Way

by James Botsford

Sandyhouse Press

ISBN: 978-0-9833110-0-3
Library of Congress Control Number: 2011903169

Copyright 2011 James Botsford

Sandyhouse Press
9004 Hollirob Lane
Wausau, Wisconsin 54403

Cover design by Jana Tappa
Book design by Sharon Thatcher

Printed in the United States by DigiCopy, Wausau, Wisconsin

Cover photo by Tenzin Botsford
Back cover photo by Dr. John Halpern

Printed on paper made in Wausau, Wisconsin

For
Tenzin and Katelin

Acknowledgements

A heartfelt thank you to Steve Moore and Steve Stolee. You guys scoured the entire text, spotting my errors and pointing out my omissions. I just want to tell you that was excruciatingly helpful.

Thanks to Phil Cousineau for permission to include a version of "My Mentor" which I wrote for his book "Once and Future Myths." Phil, your personal and exemplary enthusiasm blaze a trail for me. Thanks to Jay C. Fikes for permission to include the Foreword I wrote to his book "Reuben Snake, Your Humble Serpent." Thanks to Nora Antoine (Lakota) for permission to reprint her interview with me. Jim McKenzie, as usual your studied suggestions were nothing but good.

Thanks also to Bob Peregoy (Flathead) and the guy who wants to be called Tony. Your keen eyes and memories helped me straighten out some complicated stories.

And thank you always Mary Jo Nyenhuis for your patience and skill at making my writing look good for nearly 20 years.

And thanks mostly to Krista for your gentle and perennial support and encouragement.

You should Write that Down
Stories Along the Way

Introduction

Each of these stories I've told before – in a sauna or a car, at a kitchen table or a bar, and someone's said, "You should write that down." This book is a collection of those stories or moving snapshots from a life.

It's autobiographical and roughly chronological, but don't let that scare you.

Most of these stories were first written down in the mountains of Mexico in 2009, others in a cabin in Wisconsin in 2010. For years I resisted writing them down, wondering who would have enough time and interest to care what happened in my life. Hell, I barely have enough time to pay attention myself. My thanks to those who, over time, suggested they be saved by committing them to paper. The poems were written more contemporaneously with the times they describe.

I've tried to make these stories more about the stories than they are about me, but two things temper my success in that regard. One is that these stories are all true and I'm in them, seeing them through my eyes. The other is that I really wrote this for my son and daughter, wanting them to know more about my life as they get older, too. And, always wishing I knew more of my ancestors' stories and times, I thought to leave this record for my kids' kids.

But it's friends, mentors and colleagues who over the years, as I'd tell these stories, would laugh at the funny bits and ask good questions who helped me see the value of these verbal snapshots of a life, and hopefully thereby taught me how to tell them well. I hope they create good pictures of these times.

Skating on Thin Ice

We were 12 years old, my friend Steve Quaday and I. Steve's family lived along the Red River, out on the very south edge of Grand Forks, North Dakota. The Red River flows north. It has a reputation for being fast, dangerous, and dark reddish brown. By Steve's place it was well over a hundred feet across.

We were hockey players. That was our main sport, and we were eager for the season to start again. They hadn't yet started making ice in the outdoor rinks where we played. One cold November day after school we went down to the river below Steve's house and saw it was iced over. It was an early, clear ice, and you could see sticks and bubbles and fall leaves floating past under the surface. We tossed a little log out there and it didn't break through and the ice didn't crack. We were eager to skate.

I ran home and got my skates while Steve dug his out, and we hurried down to the riverbank and laced them up. We were a little nervous and cautious so we tried to think it through. The ice was as clear and smooth as glass and just irresistible. We thought it would be okay if we were careful.

Our plan of being careful was to start about 20 feet apart so there wouldn't be too much weight and stress in one place, and to start out by just skating straight across to the other side to see how it goes. We left sticks and pucks on the shore. So we stepped onto the ice 20 feet apart and, starting at the same time struck out for the far shore... way over there.

Nearly right away the ice started cracking under us. We could hear it and see the lightning-like veins of cracks shooting out from under our feet in all directions. We kept going. And in a few more strides it was clear that the whole sheet of surface ice was sagging under our feet. The further out we got the more it sagged, deeper and deeper, and kept cracking.

By that point we were committed. It seemed too dangerous to stop and we yelled to each other to just go faster on across. We dug in our blades with all the muscle and momentum we had in those skinny young bodies and, hearts pounding, raced to the far shore where we just dove into the bank as the cracking sounds subsided.

Catching our breath we considered our circumstance. We were now in Minnesota, a couple miles south of East Grand Forks, and a few more miles to a bridge. Up on the bank were farm fields. Way in the distance was a farmstead. It was about 30 degrees outside; the sun was going down. It would've been a long, cold walk to a farm in our skates and hooded sweatshirts. And then what? Call his parents, tell them how stupid we'd been? Ask them to make the near 20-mile round trip up to the bridge and down to get us and back home again? Were our parents even home? How would the farmer feel about us walking up in skates to use his phone (was it long distance from there)? Who wants to confess their foolhardiness to strangers? What if no one answered the phone? What if the farmer wasn't home? What if he had a mean dog? Could we even walk that far through fields in our precious skates? Would it ruin them?

We considered our options. We looked at the river across which we'd come. The ice had not broken through. The sag of the ice under our feet was gone. The tracks of our skate blades looked graceful and the whole scene looked calm – except for the water that had seeped through the cracks and now silently puddled on top of the ice, and except for the pounding of our hearts.

We looked at the pristine glassy quiet surface 50 yards down, well beyond the cracks we'd made. What if we went down there and skated back across 40 feet apart? How could we possibly die? We'd never died before, and we weren't doing anything bad.

We could see Steve's house across the river and up through the trees in North Dakota. All the options behind us in Minnesota had problems and complications, whereas if we just skated back across it could be fast and simple – the only risk being death. We considered our situation, and death seemed the least formidable of our options.

We moved 50 yards down the bank. I remember my breath being shallow and hearing my heart pound in my ears. Forty feet apart we readied ourselves. It looked far across. Because of what we now knew, the river looked like a dark abyss. Leaves and sticks and bubbles scurried by silently under the clear-as-glass ice. "Okay, one, two, three, go!"

We pushed off and gave it everything we had in a beeline for the far bank – a long way away. Just like before, lightning-like cracks split the thin ice in all directions with ragged, ominous, echoing sounds and the ice sagged more and more as we neared the center and did not give way, just crackled beneath us and ever faster we skated and the sag decreased past the center and we dove our bodies onto the home shore in a stunned pant I will never forget. And we just lay there, numb, dumb and still until we started getting too cold.

We walked to our shoes and took off our skates and headed up to Steve's house in the dimming light. We stashed our skates and went inside where his mom smiled in the kitchen and said, "Hi boys. What've you been doing?" Steve said, "Oh, we were just down by the river. What's for supper?"

You should Write that Down

*I was the lump in Mama's gravy
And the apple of her eye
She wouldn't tell the difference
And neither could I.*

The Importance of the Church

At age 13 I was sent to Confirmation class at the Presbyterian Church in Grand Forks. Our family had been sort of nominal or holiday church goers... although my father did serve as a Deacon for a long while. Confirmation class was just something that you did at that age. So I went. It was every Wednesday evening for maybe a couple of months. It was an interesting class. We did a kind of historical Bible study. Lots of good stories which I enjoyed. Some were colorful. Some mysterious. And I guess there was some discussion of belief, but what I remember were the stories and learning how to serve communion. We were supposed to assist with that after we were confirmed.

But somehow it never occurred to me that something profound was supposed to happen at the end of the class -- i.e., The Confirmation.

On the last night of the class, the instructors told us what was going to happen next Sunday. We were to show up dressed up and come before the congregation in the middle of the church service and, in repeat-after-me fashion, say that we/I accepted the Lord Jesus Christ as my lord and savior and pledging my life to God, Jesus and the Church.

That's when it hit me what this confirmation process was for. It was a preparation for joining the church and the adult circle of intentional Christians. I was stunned. My folks picked me up that cold winter night after class. I still have a visual memory of riding home in the back seat of our green Oldsmobile Delta 88, Mom and Dad in the front seat.

I said I didn't think I should go to the Confirmation on Sunday; that it just seemed too important; that I was too young to say and do anything that profoundly important. I just didn't feel ready.

My folks were shocked and scared. It was palpable. They hurriedly told me that was a bad idea; that I had to go through with it. I simply must be there. It didn't matter if I didn't understand it all, I could sort that out later. Right now the important thing was that I be there, and join the other kids in front of the church. (The church bulletins with all our names were probably already printed.)

In that dark back seat in that minute, my life changed forever. Their fearful insistence on form over substance and their disregard of my trepidation, even though at that time it was based on my sense of awe and respect for the religion, woke me up from a youthful naiveté.

I was too young to really defy them, but I was convinced I wasn't ready to do this profound thing being asked of me. So I figured a way around it that wouldn't embarrass my folks, but also respected my questioning mind. The next Sunday I put on a suit and off we went to church. When our Confirmation class was called to the front to swear our belief in Jesus, sin and salvation in front of God and the congregation, I positioned myself in the middle of the pack to avoid close scrutiny.

When we were asked to "repeat after me" in unison, I simply and silently moved my mouth open and closed in approximate cadence with the class while making sure I was neither thinking nor articulating the words.

That was as close as I ever came to becoming a Christian, although my interest in religion took me around the world more than once and resulted in both a BA and MA in the comparative study of the world's religions.

To allow fresh rain
into a temple
one must first remove the roof

Beat Foundations

By the time I was 15, I was pretty much out of control. It was '64 and I'd discovered Bob Dylan and had the extreme good fortune to be right there growing up as each new album came out (which is still somewhat true today). Moreover, I'd discovered the Beat poets. All this freed me from the terminal stability of my color-coordinated upstairs bedroom and landed me in the much more expansive, conducive and unfinished basement.

One book led to another and pretty soon I found the great writers from the Zen and Taoist traditions. Finally the world started to make a little bit of sense. This gave me strength and courage. So I started writing poetry myself.

I had (and still have) a most unique and treasured friendship with a kid my age who lived a few blocks away. Terry Fonder and I didn't usually hang out together on a daily basis, we each ran in different circles of friends. I picked a fight with him in Junior High for no good reason and he cleaned my clock in short order. It had never occurred to me that fighting could be so aggressive.

What Terry and I did best was get together for adventures. We'd steal our parents' cars for crack-of-dawn trips down gravel roads where we'd shoot at birds on telephone wires and fence posts and get the car back before anyone woke up. Or we'd see if we could get a car up to 80 mph in a residential alley in the dark. We'd drive 150 miles round trip to Fargo to get a good box of popcorn. One time we drove nonstop round trip from Grand Forks to San Diego to retrieve a couple of friends who were broke and wanted to come home.

All these adventures prepared us for our biggest one which began when we were 16. Terry was taking French his junior year and one day came up to me and suggested we go to Europe for the summer. Through the school's French Club, you could sign up for a "summer work abroad" adventure. I'd been frugal and had about three grand saved up from summer jobs, gifts and unspent allowance. Terry's mother would give him anything he asked for and his dad could be counted on to say, "Whatever your mother says."

I knew my parents couldn't stop me from doing what I wanted by this time and they knew it, too. I went to them and said something very close to this: "Which would you rather have me do this summer, buy a bigger motorcycle and take off around the country, or go to Europe through a school program and get cultured?"

Fortunately, the sponsoring organization was disorganized and what was supposed to be a home stay and work in Switzerland, wound up with us working in a cognac factory in Germany and living in a Youth Hostel. In that Hostel we met all these international travellers with tales of all these European places that turned out to be relatively accessible, all within reach. So we quit our jobs and started hitchhiking.

In those days if you had time, a little money for bread, cheese and coffee, a backpack and a sleeping bag you could get pretty much anywhere hitchhiking (although sometimes in France it was prudent to say you were Canadian).

The road was friendly, and fellow travellers had adventures and ideas to share. We wound up on the Spanish Island of Ibiza. There we found a little cave on the coast, scrounged some cardboard for the floor and moved in. I turned 17 in that cave. We lived on churos, gasseosa, cheese and jazz music from the Zodiac Bar – along with a few drinks and the remnants of the turtle soup culture from the Beats who had been there a few years ahead of us. The place was hip, but not yet hippie.

I fell ass-over-tea-kettle for a Russian woman with a very cool party apartment there. But one day the cops came and hauled her away. All they would say was that she was being deported. I watched them take her away in an open jeep from her bedroom balcony window.

We kicked around there until it was too late to make it back home for first semester of our senior year. Art, politics, jazz, hashish, continental bohemia, good coffee and a little romance here and there. We got back on the road and wound up in Amsterdam, where we split up. Terry wanted to go to Scandinavia, but I was intrigued by the road stories of North Africa.

I found a room to rent in the Kasbah of Tangier. I learned where Ginsburg, Burroughs and other Beats had lived some years before, and even was in some of those same exotic homes now kept by successor hipsters. The stoned mantra you'd hear at parties was "Katmandu for Christmas." Poems and paintings and endless mint teas around conversations on politics, religion, love and death. With the occasional puff of good kif, I was where I belonged.

But I was running out of money. I needed more money to go to India. I hadn't finished high school. I hadn't been very good about keeping in touch with my family. So I booked passage on a half cargo/half passenger Yugoslavian freighter from Casablanca to New York that would get me home by Christmas.

Meanwhile, I'd been thinking about fasting. I heard it could be a spiritual experience. I had eight days till my ship sailed. I figured if nothing else it would be a transitional purgative as I moved from one world to another. I loved the new life I'd formed, and I was leery of going back home. So I got some advice on fasting and I did it. Water only, nothing more.

A key piece of advice is to not tell people you're fasting. Especially those first four or five days where you really feel that you're going against the grain of serious habits. You could easily be persuaded to give it up if on the third day someone just said, 'Man you don't look too good. I think you better eat something.'

I remember all my senses getting very acute. It seemed like I could feel the smells I walked through, like the air was thick with them and I was breathing them in like food. When my thumb and fingertip touched, the textures were remarkable. It was a cleansing and refining time.

On the seventh night of my fast, I got on the ship and settled in to my private cabin. Something about the rocking of the ship was making a difference. A sea change in my fast, if you will. I had to lie down. Eventually I noticed my thoughts seemed to be coming from a different place. I had this perspective on myself lying there. I was present, but I was watching at the same time. As I carefully attended to this most unusual moment I began to realize that my attention was outside my body, watching the moment, the scene. I could see myself lying on the bunk, but most startling was that I could hear myself thinking, too. My thoughts and slight movements were lived in, but they were also being observed, and it was all by someone I like to call "me."

This went on for so long I eventually got bored with it, and that rocking motion of the ship had made me queasy. I started feeling sicker and weaker. I felt like I'd gotten the gift of the fast, that there was no need to push it on into being ill from the weakness and the rolling ship. So on the eighth day, following more good fasting advice, I began slowly to drink a little juice and tea, and some soup broth and take a couple of days to work back into regular fare.

13

Eight months later, after being briefly kicked out of the house, briefly expelled from school, and having made elaborate arrangements to avoid the military draft, I turned 18 on a Spanish freighter in the middle of the Atlantic on my way to India.

I promise
to hold up
the train
of circumstance
from time to time.

Hockey On and Off the Ice

Hockey, like so many other things one might pay attention to, carries well the stories of a person growing up, and the stories of a course of culture.

When I was a young kid in Grand Forks we'd play hockey in our boots in the street. We used hockey sticks and pucks so we had to protect our shins. For that we took old *Life* magazines and put them under our pants, held there by rubber bands.

A little older I joined the Park Board league; played goalie four years right up to high school; would walk about eight blocks in the dark after dinner to play, then walk back. I remember the cold and wind, but I don't remember them stopping me. We'd even shovel the ice off first if need be, just for the love of playing hockey.

I got to high school and discovered pool and snooker and, in particular, the local pool hall where I learned how to read the newspaper with a detached sarcasm. Hockey became a spectator sport on the periphery for me.

But I still enjoyed the old wooden, unheated "barn" where the UND team played. You were right near the ice, nothing in the way and a fair chance of catching a puck if you paid attention. The quality of hockey was very high and you could get hot chocolate in the warming room between periods.

My attention went elsewhere for years, but from the corner of my eye I could see the sport go goony. The Philthy Flyers (Philadelphia in the NHL) and many others, even down to younger leagues, took this most graceful sport in the direction of roller derby.

Then I started going back to UND games when I was in law school. But "the mascot issue" although not yet on the front burner, was burning my conscience. Every time I went I made a point of being back in the food area getting coffee when the announcer shouted, "Ladies and Gentlemen, here come your Fighting Sioux!" It doesn't take much to figure out the indignities there.

Here's a recipe for indignity: Move onto another culture's land and subjugate them with lies and blood. Take over. Build a bigger, newer culture that pretty much either ignores or disrespects the original culture here. In your institution of "higher learning" make a caricature of the conquered people and take them as your mascot for your pleasure and amusement. Then, with your team of white guys in your arena where the local white folks can afford tickets and cheer them on (think gladiators) you take pride in "your Fighting Sioux." But we're not done yet. No, the indignity is not complete until one more step is taken. When the Indians at the school and on the reservations tell the school leaders that caricaturing them as a mascot is a travesty and an insult, it is then the school and community leaders have the audacity to tell the Indians that the Indians are once again on the losing end and wrong. That, in fact, using them as a mascot is a way of honoring them. Now the indignity is complete. Now we have placed the cherry on the steaming pile of shit.

One more dimension of this story needs to be told. It is the Englestad Arena. I'll tell it shorter than I should; shorter than it is. There was a wealthy alumni businessman who had long ago been a back-up goalie at UND. His name was Ralph Englestad, and he'd made it big as a casino owner in Las Vegas where he was known for his fight against unions and his curious interest in Nazi memorabilia. For reasons of his own he decided to spend about $100 million to build "the best hockey arena in the world" on property next to the UND campus, and after some twists and turns the project began in the name of a "charity" Englestad created which then leased the property from the state of North Dakota for one dollar per year for 30 years. All this was developing while the mascot issue was flaring up.

There was one key qualifier in Mr. Englestad's generous offer: he really wanted UND to keep the "Fighting Sioux" mascot, logo, etc. Because the mascot issue was a hot one (schools all over the country were dropping their Indian mascots), and because it had caused some ugliness at UND with allegations of racism, the President of UND appointed a very diverse Commission to study the issue and list the pros and cons of the mascot issue. He said his decision on the mascot would be informed by the Commission's findings since they were to be so thorough and cross-cultural.

After an unnecessarily long and thorough study, the Commission was ready to report to the President of the University. On the eve of the issuance of the Report, Mr. Englestad called up a member of the State Board of Higher Education. That Board has authority over the state schools, including UND, but up till then had indicated they would stay back and let the University President and his Commission process reach a solution.

Englestad told that Board member that if they didn't intervene, fast and hard, and decree compliance with Englestad's view of the Fighting Sioux, he was taking his money and going home. He said that even though he'd already invested $10 million and the steel skeletal structure was standing out there on prime prairie property, he didn't give a shit. He'd let it stand there and rust away. It was an ultimatum. If you want the money, you intervene and force the logo and mascot to remain, damn the Commission or the merits...or the ethics for that matter. A nasty letter to this effect was sent by Englestad to the University President at the same time.

Well, just when you'd hope for a happy ending on the moral high ground where decision makers would do the right thing and North Dakotans could be proud of their state's integrity in the history books to come... just about then you'd be hugely and tragically disappointed.

What happened next was that the State Board of Higher Education "met" the next day and capitulated. They took the money. They blinked. They thwarted the dignified, thoughtful, inclusive, democratic Commission process. They usurped the multiyear process at the campus. They trumped everything in a fit of anxious short-sightedness. They sold out the good people and good name of North Dakota for a bag of Vegas silver.

I've been in this new arena. Inside the main entrance there is a giant face of an Indian in expensive marble from India. The face is in the floor where everyone who walks in there steps on it. Upstairs, where the fancy suites are, there's a richly carpeted hallway that runs around that whole level of the arena connecting all the private suites. Woven into that carpet is the face of an Indian every few feet. In order not to step on those faces you have to walk like a kid on a sidewalk trying not to step on a crack so as not to break his mother's back.

All these power shenanigans in North Dakota did not co-opt the National Collegiate Athletic Association (NCAA) from their broader responsibility. The NCAA was in the process of a national study of this thorny mascot issue at this time, and concluded that about 20 of their participating schools around the country had mascot names and/or logos that were "hostile and abusive." The Fighting Sioux were in the cross hairs on that list.

The NCAA did not (nor could they) say the school

had to change its mascot and logo. But they did say that a school could neither play in nor host NCAA sanctioned play-off games if it had "hostile or abusive" mascots that the local affected Indian tribes objected to. Moral persuasion wasn't working at UND, but money did seem to get their attention so the NCAA position had some power.

The "best arena in the country" was hoping to bring in a lot of money hosting play-offs in the out years. So this NCAA ruling stung them in their wallet and their misplaced sense of pride. In fact, the proponents of "their" Fighting Sioux were so tenaciously offended that they sued the NCAA for being too heavy handed.

The lawsuit was settled with a stipulation that said the "Fighting Sioux" mascot could stay if the two local Sioux tribes in North Dakota would agree that the name and logo were acceptable now and would be for at least another 30 years. This had to occur by a date certain in 2009. So out came the wallets, the promises, the attempts to influence tribal elections. It wasn't pretty. They did manage to get a lukewarm endorsement from one tribe, but not from the other. They got the court to grant an extension for one more year.

In 2010 they ran out of time. Hopefully, the issue is dead. UND created task groups and committees to retire the logo "with respect," find a new one and retool the marketing. The marble Indian face in the floor will remain as a sad artifact of a bad story, but the less permanent indicia of "The Fighting Sioux" was given a must-be-gone date of August 15, 2011. The merchandise and paraphernalia are enjoying a marketing surge.

Hockey when it's done right is the most fluid and graceful of team sports.

POSTSCRIPT

*"Some things last longer than you think they will
There are some kind of things you can never kill."*
Bob Dylan, "Cold Irons Bound"

Just when I thought this story had reached an end, members of the North Dakota state legislature, including the House Majority Leader, have introduced three separate bills that attempt to forbid the University or the State Board of Higher Education from dropping the Fighting Sioux logo and mascot. Then the state's Attorney General said such a law would violate the state's Constitution. So did that end this ridiculously bizarre story? Nope. In response to the Attorney General the House Majority Leader said they would then attempt to amend the state's Constitution.

I assure the reader I'm not smoking any funny cigarettes today or making a silly attempt at social satire. I'm just reporting the news in the year 2011.

Agot's Finger

When I was 16 I became friends with a guy who was 18. He was a big guy, football player. I was a skinny guy, pool shooter. His name was Dick Agotness, "Agot" to his friends. Not sure how we became such good buddies, but we hung out a lot. Used to get a six pack and jump in his '57 Chevy and drive around. Often we'd wind up parked on a gravel road a few miles outside of town listening to the radio and drinking beer.

Lotta guys were getting drafted then, the Vietnam War was hot. We'd talk a lot about how bad it was, how wrong and riddled with hypocrisy, how the poor kids had to fight it mostly cuz they couldn't get draft deferments as easily.

Agot graduated, but he wasn't going to college. His family didn't have much money, and he didn't really want to go anyway. So he was pretty nervous about the draft.

One Saturday night we were parked on a gravel road south of town; just me, Agot and a six pack. After a while he said he got his draft notice. He was classified 1-A, and he was supposed to report in a month or so. We commiserated and talked about options. We said that war wasn't worth dying for, especially not this one.

Then Agot looked at me and asked me to chop off his trigger finger. We weren't sure if not having a trigger finger would keep you out, but we figured if it wouldn't, then probably the fact that you chopped it off to keep from going would keep you out.

Agot had an older uncle he really admired. I think it was because his Uncle Clarence was unique, and never fit much in the main stream. Clarence owned some farmland which he rented out for income, and Clarence, who liked to drink considerably, lived at that time in the basement of a cheap hotel in Grand Forks where you could rent by the week or month. Agot was always bringing up some philosophical gem Clarence had told him. It was usually something that was perceptive and would make us laugh.

So when Agot asked me to chop off his finger and told me he'd brought a hatchet that was in the trunk and that he wanted to do it right now when we were feeling the beer... well, I had a little hesitation. I told him that although I was sure our view of the war being wrong was right, I just felt that since I was only 16 and half drunk I didn't feel qualified to do something so permanent and decisive.

But I didn't say no. I told Agot to go talk it over with someone older, someone he respected and could trust. I said if after having done that he still wanted me to chop off his trigger finger, I'd sure enough do it. Agot said he'd go talk to Uncle Clarence.

Agot never brought it up again, and pretty soon he was gone into the Army. Agot was one of those unfortunate young guys who never really came all the way back from the war. He was remote, aloof, liked to party, bought a loud chopped Harley and never planned beyond the day. When offered an idea, he'd often say, "it's your world, I'm just bivouacin'."

At first he wasn't too bad. Then I took off for a year or two and when I saw him again he had the shakes a little and part of his conversation was just with himself. I wasn't in Grand Forks a lot in the ensuing years, so when I'd go back and see him the deterioration was very pronounced. He'd been in and out of VA hospitals. They had him on a variety of medications, primarily intended to address his mental condition. Eventually, over a number of years, he turned ashen gray, ground his teeth down to near nothing, couldn't carry on a conversation except with himself, didn't know what drugs he was taking, was living in a homeless shelter, and eventually died before he hit 40.

Although I thought I made a considered and open-minded decision that night on the gravel road when the hatchet was in the trunk – if I knew then what I know now, I sure would've chopped that finger off right then and there.

Agot

Agot, dull buzz nerves drunken and exposed
hidden in a swirl
where did you go
where is your home of alienation and sadness
where do you go.
Aggie, you made it
to that dark deep romantic
death you choose to imitate and tease.
Uncle Clarence thinks he's the saddest man alive
and the only one who knows it and
he cries when you look up to him
and you loving each other for it.
Agot and Clarence buying a farm
so they'll have some place to leave
and some place to go for awhile to mourn losing
the farm.
So little means so much.
Aggie why do you go
to she who says no?
and why do you stay so long?
I know you told her everything
you could never forget and
she forgot it overnight all alone
and I might have guessed you'd be gone by then
in a glazed-eyed stare
repeating it all everywhere-
keeping yourself surrounded
with reasons not to make a move
and people who deserve
to be free of each other.

The Frenchman

We were 16 and trying to hitchhike from Barcelona, Spain, to Basel, Switzerland, to see two pretty girls who worked in a tourist agency. My friend, Terry Fonder, was my travelling partner at the time, and we'd had pretty good luck hitching everywhere. The only place it was unusually hard was France. So once we got inside France and found it tough to catch a ride together we decided to split up and meet in Basel.

Sure enough, it worked. We put a hundred yards between us and Terry got a ride right away. After trying most of the day, in the late afternoon a guy on a motorcycle stopped for me. He was about 50 years old and said he was going all the way to Lyon, where he lived. That was incredible luck to get such a long ride, even though it meant we'd be on the road till midnight. Indeed, it was even later because every hour or two we'd stop at a roadhouse and take turns buying each other a glass of wine. We had no language in common, but enjoyed each other's company. The fine open ride through the French countryside and the wine took the night chill off.

About two a.m. we pulled into what I'd call a tin hut slum somewhere in Lyon and parked the bike in front of his little one room house. I started to roll my bag out on the floor but he insisted the floor was hard and cold and the bed was big enough. The bed felt great, the guy smelled like my Grandfather (a smell I liked and a man I missed), and I fell asleep reliving my good fortune of the day and the promise that in the morning he'd take me to the edge of the city where the highway left for Basel.

At dawn something pulled me out of a deep sleep. I was sleeping on my stomach and disoriented by the strangeness and then realized he was on top of me with his cock between my legs. I rolled over in disbelief and started to speak, but he put his finger to his lips and pleaded with me to allow him one more minute. I squeezed my legs together.

It might've been his kindness and generosity of the day before, it might've been the sad loneliness in his face, it might've been my confidence that he wouldn't hurt me. It might've been all those things together that resulted in me just laying there with my legs squeezed together while he let some spit fall from his mouth to the space between my pinched legs, and then worked his cock there until he came.

I didn't hate him. I didn't much like him anymore, and was sadly disappointed in the turn this good story had taken, but I didn't hate him. Further sleep was out of the question so we got up and, like he promised, he took me on his motorcycle to the edge of Lyon to where there was a good place to hitchhike toward Basel.

I stood a long time that morning trying to get a ride; trying to sort out what happened and what it meant. Best I could figure it meant I was strong, had compassion in my heart, a good sense of what would and wouldn't hurt me, and it meant that I was very much heterosexual.

Overland to India

WHY INDIA?

rowing up in the suburban world of North Dakota in the '60's, India was to me shining like a diamond in a billy goat's ass.

I had an admittedly somewhat naïve image of India as being permeated by spiritual sensibility and a vast capacity for tolerance. But I wasn't all wrong. In India, at least at that time, there was a remarkable deference and respect afforded to actions, beliefs, life style, clothing, music . . . anything really that was perceived as having a sincere religious root.

I think it comes in part from the inclusiveness of the spiritual traditions that were born in India. None of this stark "my way or the highway" bullshit you see in so much of the current manifestations of the great religions that came out of the desert (Judaism, Christianity, Islam).

Although most of the cultural homes of Buddhism now are elsewhere, Buddhism's original home is India. And the Hindus have a generosity of recognition that encompasses wisdom from wherever it's found.

I remember thinking at the time that the whole circus of human possibility was happening in India everyday, and most every manifestation of spiritual possibility, no matter how strange, was at the very least accommodated if not flat-out accorded respect.

I found this image of India to be very appealing and enticing. I was aware of the poverty, the over-population, the injustices of the caste system and the byzantine bureaucracies that I still think they got primarily from the British. But regardless, if there were viable spiritual paths happening, I figured they were probably going on somewhere in India, where people took these things seriously.

I was a teenager. I wasn't just looking for answers. I was also looking for questions. I wanted it all. I felt that strongly, and given that internally propelled proclivity it seemed to me that India was the best place to go. And part of the tremendous value of going there was the bursting of the bubbles of the preconceived illusions I had of the place. I mean it was just about perfect for me at that time. At least that's the way I look at it.

Coming of age what do you want to know? Well, everything. In my case that included a main emphasis on wisdom. It just seemed to me the thing most worth pursuing. So where to go to do that? Well, at my age and in my time India seemed the best place to start. And so by God that's where I was going.

THE PREPARATIONS

With careless disregard for the feelings of my parents, I took off for India without saying goodbye. I was almost 18 at the time, and they did know I was planning to leave. Maybe it's unfair to myself to call it careless disregard. Maybe it just would've been too painful to see the hurt and concern in my mother's eyes and the disappointment in my dad's.

Anyway, other than saying goodbye properly, I certainly had the courage to go. I'd taken off for Europe at 16, turned 17 on Ibiza, wound up renting an apartment in the Medina in Tangiers when my friends were doing their first semester senior year. So when I came home around Christmas at 17, I had a few specific ideas in mind. One was to finish high school. One was to avoid the draft. The third was to figure out how to get myself to India, overland so as to see where I was going.

Cramming my senior year into one semester was easy once we got past an initial crisis. Maybe it was because the war wasn't going well, maybe because of the protestors, or maybe just some common sabre rattling rally-round-the-flag notion. ("Your country, right or wrong," my dad used to say.) Whatever precipitated it, Central High School in Grand Forks, North Dakota had, while I was in the Moroccan Kasbah paying attention to other things, instituted a policy requiring all students to stand and pledge allegiance to the wall during first hour after the National Anthem blared over the loudspeakers.

Well, I just wasn't going to do that. Unfortunately, I had one of the coaches for first hour and he was equally adamant that I was. So it was down to the Principal's office where, after hours of meetings with all concerned, it was determined that I would be expelled. Just before the deal was done though, the psychology teacher who they'd had me meet with earlier, came in and said he had an idea. What if I promised not to be in the building during first hour? That would satisfy the school's main articulated argument which was that my defiance would be disruptive (maybe they meant contagious). And it would allow me to complete high school.

The logic was too much for my opponents and they had to acquiesce, but only after threatening me that if I was on the school property during first hour I would indeed be expelled. When the dust settled, my friends asked me what was the result of all this consternation and flurries of meetings of officials. I told them the result was that I got to sleep in an extra hour every day for the whole semester.

The second thing I wanted to do was avoid the draft. I was unequivocally opposed on moral, political and spiritual grounds. I wouldn't go. However, I wanted to get out of it in a way that best kept my freedom and my options open. So I combined this effort with getting to India. The two just came together nicely.

It was 1967 and Uncle Sam wasn't very fussy about who got drafted. I remembered that years earlier I'd fallen out of a tree and an x-ray of my back showed I had a vertebra that was moving laterally a little.

I went back to the doctor, who was Chair of the North Dakota Republican Party. He was a man of integrity and generosity of spirit, besides being a damn fine surgeon. I told him I had lots of plans and ideas for my life and none of them included getting drafted to fight this war. We took an x-ray of my back and compared it to the one taken years earlier when I'd fallen from the tree. He took very careful measurements and showed me with a pencil tip how far that vertebra had moved. I asked if it had moved enough to keep me out of the draft. He said no.

I asked if that combined with my polio at age three was enough. He said he was very familiar with the draft, and that under normal circumstances yes, those two factors combined would likely keep me out – but not now, when the military was taking pretty much anyone they could get and lowering their standards.

The doc said that because that vertebra was moving toward my spinal column, sooner or later I'd have to have surgery to stop it. And if I let it get too bad, it could slip in such a way that I'd be paralysed.

Using that same pencil tip, I said what about if it slipped this much more? Would that keep me out but not be imminently dangerous?

What I knew (or thought I knew) that he may not have known was that there was a little crack of light getting in through the ironclad draft registration system. What I understood was this: every young man had to register for the draft within five days of turning 18, and if you registered in the U.S. you could then only leave with your draft board's permission and must return when they called you (and the penalties were harsh). But if, upon turning 18, you registered within five days at a U.S. Embassy in a foreign country you were free to stay gone and not subject to the draft board until you returned of your own volition.

To this day, I don't recall how I knew this, or if, in fact, it was ever even true. But this understanding of the military draft propelled me to some serious decision making.

So the good doctor put the pencil tip where he thought it would keep me out of the draft but not likely put me at high, immediate risk of paralysis.

I had about eight months to go before I turned 18. So, while finishing school I got a job moving furniture. This combined my goals vis-à-vis the draft and my desire to make enough money to go to India. Although carrying a large load to cram the senior year into one semester, I worked a lot - after school and weekends. Ironically, the local mover I worked for had the contract to move military families into and out of the local air base so there was plenty of opportunity for overtime.

About every six weeks I went back to the doctor for another x-ray. We tracked the movement of my vertebra. Meanwhile, I booked a berth on a Spanish freighter that was sailing from New York to San Sabastian, Spain on a timetable that would have me turn 18 in the middle of the Atlantic Ocean.

Shortly before my departure date the doctor took a last picture, saying he figured the army wouldn't want me now. I asked him to put that series of x-rays in chronological order, along with my earlier polio record and a cover letter from him and send it to my local draft board on my birthday.

That he did, and five days after my 18th birthday I walked in to the American Embassy in Madrid, saying, "How do you do? I'm here to register for the draft."

Dawn Rolls 'Round the World

Dawn in its breathing freshness
warms the busy dew
on the sloping meadow and the
forested shore.
We speak in sequence one long song
crystalline and soft.
Dawn's long shadows slowly expand
giving traceless patterns
to the fullness of day
in which for all you breathe
patiently.
Days helpless and hopeful
days hopeless and helpful
richly woven like the forested shore
play in the sweet dusty meadows.
In a dance of leaves
in a breeze of trees
the fresh breath of dawn
warms what it can reach.

THE OVERLAND TRIP

Overland to India proved a complicated affair. First, after registering for the draft I went back to Tangier to explore the notion of buying a donkey and riding as far as Egypt. Over a period of a month or two in Tangier shopping for a donkey and doing other fun and simple things, that plan got nixed. It was partly because I was told I'd never get into Israel from Egypt with all those fresh Arab passport stamps, and partly because I sensed somewhere within that this might be pushing things a bit too far.

So along comes this psychologist from the U.S. with a 500 cc Triumph motorcycle, a desire to get to northern Europe and very little money. We got along and were both traveling light so we agreed I'd go along on the bike and buy gas till we got to Paris where I was planning to jump on the fabled Orient Express.

Well, we managed a fine side trip up through Portugal and when coming back across northern Spain, somewhere near Burgos, we had a serious accident involving a large truck. I remember skipping down the highway like a stone on water.

After the accident an ambulance came and hauled me back to the local provincial capitol of Burgos. I was pretty beat up and hurting, and half out of it. The ambulance stopped at the emergency entrance of the closest hospital and they pulled the gurney out. The ambulance driver had one end of the bed and the hospital guy had the other. An argument ensued over who was going to pay for what. It was like a tug of war with me on the bed. It didn't get resolved, so they put me and the gurney back in the ambulance and the driver took me to another hospital across town where they took me in.

This was right around dusk at dinner time and this male nurse took the head of my bed on wheels while finishing what he was chewing and tried to talk to me as he wheeled me down the hall. I remember his smile and that pieces of food were falling out of his mouth onto my face.

He got me into a room and onto a bed and did a cursory cleaning of the blood from my wounds. Somewhere in this process, I realized he was a flaming gay; might've been when he moved the bloody washcloth to my genitals and giggled. Anyway, he then started to suture my cuts which were still obviously full of gravel and dirt. I refused to let him do it, a doctor was called and two other nurses were brought in to clean my wounds and stitch me up.

In the morning the psychologist showed up. Fortunately, he hadn't been hurt bad and even more fortunately for me he had my gear and found me. I told him to get me out of there and stick me on a train for Madrid. He found a wheelchair, got me dressed and wheeled me out the front door of the hospital without us ever stopping to check either in or out.

We got in a taxi and went to the train station. He offered, very apologetically, to accompany me. I said there was no point in him accompanying me on a train headed south, and that since he was already near broke and headed north, he better keep going that way. We parted friends and I can't even remember his name.

The angel on the train who spotted my wounded predicament and gave me generous amounts of pain pills also got me to the British American Hospital in Madrid. There I spent 10 days sharing a room with a dying old Dutchman named Mr. Ripon. Mr. Ripon had been living alone in Madrid a long time and for too much of that time had lived on brandy and milk. He saw things others didn't. He was a sweet old man, but sometimes in the middle of our conversations, he'd stop and introduce me to someone who had just come into the room. Neither I nor the nurses ever saw any of those guests he had.

There was a Spanish doctor who was in charge of my care the 10 days I was in the hospital. He was wonderful. By the end, he knew my story and said how much he respected the trip I was on. He said he would see to it I could leave the hospital without paying a single peseta. He said that some day, after my trip when I got home, maybe I would send him some payment. Regrettably, I lost his name along the way and was never able to track him down to repay his skilful kindness. All I can do now these decades later is acknowledge him here with my continuing respect and gratitude.

After 10 days in the British American Hospital, I was released with a cast on my right leg from my toes to my hip. In an effort to conserve money I rented a large linen closet on the 5th floor of a walk-up for $25/month. There was a small bed in there and, as it evolved, the landlady (who lived elsewhere) sublet it back from me for $5/month for the right to take naps there in the mid-afternoon. The stuff of life.

Music, good coffee, local culture (e.g. paella and steam baths) and a beautiful senorita kept me near Plaza del Sol in Madrid for months after my cast came off. But eventually I went north and caught the Orient Express and rode it clear through to Istanbul.

Shortly before I left Madrid I got a letter forwarded from my local draft board. In the envelope was my draft card. It said I was classified "4-F". This classification was at that time the crown jewel of deferments. The joke was that 4-F meant they'd call you just after they called women and children.

Istanbul, like Tangier, is a crossroads of continents. These are unique energy places where whole continents funnel down to pass through before opening up into the next continent. Hour glasses of the world. As such, there's very little that hasn't been seen or done in these wondrous cities. They have a capacity, born of centuries of experience, for understanding most everything human nature manifests.

The fact that they're relatively welcoming, universal and non-judgmental does not, however, mean they're not a bit dangerous, but I've never had any serious trouble in either city. I've been twice to Istanbul for about a month in all, and thrice to Tangier for about five months in all. Each trip to each city enriched me.

As you travel the world, especially on the cheap, you discover that there are streams of relatively like-minded travellers out and about, and they're often coming from or going to the same places as others in this stream – mayhaps yourself. There are places they tend to gravitate toward, maybe to rest up, or to take in something unique and worth the effort. In these places (whether they are cities, islands, mountain towns or beaches) you can learn a lot about what's going on where you're going. Such a place is Istanbul, where I learned my idea of hitchhiking from there to India was not likely to work, and for a very good reason: no cars. This was January of 1968 and there just wasn't much private traffic. Most all the trucks and buses were local or regional, and most of the little trucks and cars were local and loaded to the gills. There were a few big fancy, long road buses, but they were in it for speed and efficiency and they were expensive. They weren't for me. There were also a couple of big colorful hippie buses – double-deckers starting from London. They weren't for me either, so I took a second class train into eastern Turkey till it ran out of tracks. Then I started taking local buses, one town to the next.

It was January of 1968 when I headed across the Bosporus, east out of Istanbul. The U.S. was launching some of its air war in Vietnam out of a base in Turkey. As I recall the world had recently learned of the clandestine bombing raids in Cambodia and Laos. Truth was trickling in. At any rate, the whole ugly mess was very unpopular around the world, and the Turks were particularly pissed about the Americans using this air base in Turkey to perpetrate belligerent mayhem.

I was on a local bus in eastern Turkey. The bus was half empty; it was winter cold and blustery, snow in the hills and some of the bus windows were broken out, and by that I mean gone. There was only one source of heat on this bus. In the aisle in the middle of the bus was a square cornered five gallon metal pail. In the pail were a little kerosene and some kerosene-soaked sticks. The seats around this scene were all darkly charred and empty.

I was wearing pretty much everything I had and was freezing. Those tough country Turks were all bundled up too (better than me). But once in awhile it would get so cold on the bus that even the Turks couldn't stand it. There'd be a discussion and then someone would throw a match into the kerosene can and we'd have a very stinky open fire throwing off heat as we rattled down the rough road. After awhile the fumes would get so bad I was alternately spitting in a handkerchief and trying to breathe through that and sticking my head out a broken window for fresh air and to relieve the stinging in my eyes. Eventually it would get so bad that even the Turks couldn't take it anymore, so someone would throw something over the top of the can to smother the fire. This routine of back and forth extremes went on all day. I was the only non-Turk on the bus, and the only English speaker. At some point in the late afternoon the conversation got heated. I was picking up key words like "America," "Johnson," (U.S. President), and it was clear these guys were pissed about the war, the U.S. duplicity and the use of a Turkish base for nefarious purposes. The anger was palpable. Then came a critical moment. I could tell the guy behind me was trying to get my attention, but I played dumb till he gave my shoulder a shove. I turned around to face him and the bus went silent. He pointed a thick calloused finger at me and asked, "American?" I nodded affirmatively and said, "Yes, American." He took that finger and drew it across his throat and as he did so said, "Johnson, czzzzzzk!" with an angry toothy grin. In a fluke of brilliance with all eyes on me I had the presence of mind to draw my own finger across my throat baring my teeth and said, "Yes, Johnson, czzzzzk!"

There were a couple more seconds of silence to digest the moment and then laughter and a few pats on my back and handshakes. After that I felt very safe with these fellows and we bounced on into a little town at dusk. End of the line for this bus, but another would go on further east in the morning.

I made a mental note that the next time a situation

like that arose, I was going to say I was Canadian. The whole trip was exhilarating, eye-opening and engendered in me a healthy respect for cultural variety. The buses were cheap, sometimes crowded, but there was always a meal and a bed in some mud-walled town at the end of the day.

This way of moving got me from Istanbul, through Turkey, Iran, Afghanistan, Pakistan and down to New Delhi in about three weeks. Although it seems impossible, my recollection is that my bus fares for all across there totalled around $30. Can that be right? I recall it from my travel notes. But my notes, alas, went through the Flood of '97 in Grand Forks, where I'd thought they'd be safe on the top shelf of the fruit room in my parents' basement.

I mentioned this stream of folks on the path of worldwide wayfarers who you bump into periodically though you're not traveling together. Such was my connection to Proloy Chatterji. Proloy's family is Hindu, but they got bumped out of what's now Pakistan in "The Partition." Proloy was an artist who had gone to Germany and was on his way back home. We first spoke in Istanbul. I saw him in Tehran where we were in the same hotel for a few days. Then in Afghanistan I met him again in Herat, and we overlapped in Kandahar as I recall. Then in Kabul, enjoying the great Bazaar and resting up for the push through the Khyber Pass and on into Pakistan, Proloy confided that he'd just learned that due to the India/Pakistan conflict-of-the-month, the Pakistanis wouldn't allow Indians to travel through their country. He was almost out of money and stuck. I lent him enough to fly from Kabul to Delhi and he assured me he would make it right when I came to his home there.

That's how I came to acquire my "second family." I eventually made my way by more cheap local buses on into Lahore and then a rough 3d class train to New Delhi and the Chatterji home. There I was welcomed like a hero.

Paying me back was just the beginning. They insisted I stay on and on, insisted I return, included me like family in their great Indian philosophical oratorical events of the extended family through feasts.

Children of that extended family have remained friends of my family, and through deaths and marriages we still feel welcome to visit each other in our respective corners of the world and be taken in as family.

I remember with particular fondness taking my wife to their home many years later. Shortly after we were married we decided to go to India for a year – partly to see if we were compatible enough through thick and thin to bring children into the world. We figured if we could survive in India for a year and still want to make babies together, the chances were good we'd stay together and raise them in a way we both believed in. That was a dozen years after my first visit, and although I'd been back once in-between while working on my Master's in World Religions, I wasn't sure how they'd welcome a new member of our "extended family." Not to worry, they took to Krista instantly and insisted we stay on with them. We did so, making their home our base camp for the year as we travelled around India and its environs (Kashmir, Ladakh, Sikkim, Nepal). I remember Delhi being so hot sometimes that you couldn't sleep indoors. We'd dump water on the concrete roof in the evening to cool it off and eventually, around midnight, it was possible to lay out a bed and sleep up there until the first rays of sun hit us, and not a minute more. But by that time, someone would've made "first chai" and the world looked good again.

IN INDIA

India was, for me at that time, an even richer experience than I had hoped – albeit in unexpected ways (just as you might expect).

On the one hand, my youthful notion of a spiritual aura permeating the country was a bubble ripe for the bursting and burst it did a thousand times.

On the other hand, religious tolerance, respect for spiritually motivated living was there in spades, almost taken for granted. The cow had the right-of-way even in the outdoor market. A naked-but-for-ashes sadhu could walk through Connaught Place in the heart of New Delhi without attracting a crowd – to say nothing of a cop.

India is not immune to "spiritual materialism" to be sure. There are shills and charlatans and lechers and thieves. But there is also much more serious and accommodated spiritual inquiry than you will find most anywhere else in the world. At least it sure worked for me at the time. I found ample ways to study in books, in ashrams, on mountain tops, in late night informal conversations in tea houses and buses. India was a welcoming land of vast capacities. I hope that's still true.

ON THE RETURN

I had a particularly tense moment on the return trip from India toward Istanbul which was just flat-out stupid of me in retrospect. I decided that rather than retracing my route I'd see some new country. So when I left India and got to Lahore, Pakistan, instead of heading northwest toward the Khyber Pass, Kabul and on back through Afghanistan, I'd go south and cross the arid desert of southern Pakistan and come up through southern Iran to Tehran. From Tehran west to Istanbul there was only really one direct route, so this first half of the trip was my chance for a change.

Again I was looking for cheap local buses to save money, to get a sense of local people and customs and to see the country in a slower, more connected way.

By late afternoon the first day out we were well out into

dry desert country. Sometimes it was hard to tell where the road was. The bus had a lot of rough hewn but affable men on it and periodically stopped to pick up more. I assumed they were all Pakistanis, but later determined that may not have been the case. Many of these guys had rugged wooden bird cages filled with birds. Others who seemed to be traveling with them had big mysterious tied bundles.

Again I was the only English speaker on the bus, so was limited to little pantomime conversations. By late afternoon in this hot dusty bus on an unpaved route, I was really hoping for a stop and had an urgent need to pee. The urge to pee can become obsessive, especially when it seems there is no opportunity for relief. Such must've been my state of mind for it is the only way I can explain what happened next.

As I was trying to examine my options: piss in my pants, or in my shoe or ask someone for an empty water bottle, and how crudely obvious it would be – well, right about then the bus stopped, seemingly in the middle of nowhere. All the guys got off and walked over to a little ridge, spread out facing away from the bus and squatted down. Perfect, I thought, for this is how men pee in the pantaloons they mostly wore. I followed them out of the bus and went and joined the line of men all facing the same direction. I unzipped my pants and as I was about to urgently pee, some guy next to me said, "Pssst," and whispered something unintelligible with a wild look in his eyes.

All of a sudden it was like I woke up and realized we were all facing Mecca and this was evening prayer. I quickly got myself together and hurried off behind them not stopping till I was out of sight on the other side of the bus. I don't know how many on that bus knew what I almost did, but I never felt any repercussions.

That was the tense part, but let me finish the story. In the middle of the next afternoon, the bus again stopped seemingly at a random spot, only this time most of the guys (maybe a dozen) who I now figured for smugglers, gathered their bird cages and bundles and struck off walking north toward what looked like some sort of walled compound way off in the distance.

Those of us remaining on the bus (maybe ten of us) resumed our journey toward the Iranian border. Just before dark we pulled up to a series of about six plain square mud huts with dirt floors. A family lived in one of them and the others were empty. Through stumblebum communications with universal signals, I learned the following: this is the last outpost on the Pakistani side, and as far as this bus goes. Once a week an Iranian bus comes down, crosses the border which is a few miles away and comes to pick up whoever is here in these huts waiting to cross into Iran. The Iranian bus had been here yesterday. So I had six days to wait. The family living there cooked for all of us on an outdoor clay fireplace. The costs were nominal. The food was simple but good: rice, spinach, yogurt, mutton or goat, oranges and tea with sugar. I unrolled my sleeping bag on the floor of a hut. I remember noticing there were no chairs anywhere in this enclave. Time passed.

Six days later, sure enough, we saw a cloud of dust in the distance in the morning and a bus approached, loaded us up, and took us to the customs post and on into Iran to the first big town, which was as far as that bus went. The next morning early I walked down to the bus station to catch a bus toward Tehran and sure enough there, squatting against a wall in the sun, waiting for a bus north, were all the smugglers with their birds and bundles. We pointed at each other and had a good laugh of recognition.

POSTSCRIPT

When I got back to the States I went back to see my doctor. He took some new x-rays, compared them to the old and said that eventually surgery was inevitable. He recommended I do it now while I was still a teenager (18) because my body would heal better. I didn't really have anything to do at the time except read and think so we did it. In the decades since, I've had a good strong back, and always been able to do my share of heavy lifting.

Equanimity

One of the singularly most important
things I ever learned
was how to be equanimous
no matter what's going on
inside or out.

These are wisdom teachings
power teachings
warrior teachings
Buddhist and Taoist teachings
the way I learned them
from Vipassana and Han Shan.

Wouldn't want to be on this road
without access to equanimity
but I don't want to live there
I want to know how to get there
when I need to
in a hurry.

But give me the Roly Poly
the vicissitudes
the ups and downs
the full joys and sorrows
I'll pay the price of a little anger and pain
as a ticket to the dance
if I can leave my equanimity
at the door.

Dam Dumb

It's peculiar how one can be described as "wise beyond his years" one day, then turn around and do something really stupid the next. And sometimes two heads are dumber than one.

I didn't know Kip O'Leary very well, although his brother, Donovan, and I were good friends. Kip was home for the summer from school somewhere. It was in our college years so we really should've known better. These were lazy days – plenty of energy and curiosity, but better to be broke than working.

The Red Lake River comes wandering through northwestern Minnesota, first south from the Red Lake Indian Reservation, then back around in a northwesterly direction till it flows into the Red River of the North, which is the Minnesota/North Dakota border clear on up to Manitoba. But before these rivers merge, back upstream there's a man made dam on the Red Lake River. The river at that point is over a hundred feet wide, and there's about a ten foot vertical drop over the dam. It's a little pushy.

I was living in a little house along the river at the time, a couple miles downstream from the dam. One day Donovan and Kip stopped over and noticed my canoe in the yard. I wasn't a whitewater kind of guy so I had a canoe designed for camping and fishing on lakes. It was a heavy 17' fiberglass boat with three keels, which made it steady in the wind on a big open lake, but not very maneuverable.

I don't recall if Donovan had somewhere else to be or just didn't like the feel of our idea, but Kip and I made a plan to paddle on the Red Lake River the next day starting at the dam.

The next day we met at the dam where you can park a car and launch a boat either a hundred yards upstream or a little ways downstream. We started out pretty smart. My dad taught me to do the hardest part first, so we put in above the dam and paddled upstream for an hour or so, then turned and paddled back down to the take-out. It was a lovely day and up till then there was no indication we were going to do anything particularly dangerous and stupid.

Before we put the canoe back on my car roof, we walked over and looked at the dam – like moths to a flame. The roar was enticing, as was the volume of water piling up at the bottom of the dam in a loud curling chaos of physics and foam.

There at the dam we had to stand close and talk loud to hear each other. A notion emerged. If we did it just right we could make it over the dam and through the wild high froth at the bottom. The water looked to be just a few inches deep as it rushed over the dam in a slick hurry. We might scrape, but if we had enough momentum and were perfectly upright when we hit it, we ought to go straight over.

The real problem was the bottom. There was a log as big as a person rolling and tumbling at the bottom, and sometimes it would get pushed and sucked under and re-main out of sight for many seconds, only to pop back up still caught in the action and roll and tumble some more. There was no way to know how long that log had been tumbling in there. There were also some branches and chunks of concrete and stone here and there in the splash.

But there was an area, about a third of the way across, where the course looked clear. In that span of about 15 feet there were no discernable obstacles. If we had enough speed … and we hit it just right … but what if we didn't?

What if we flipped? What if we wound up with the canoe and two bodies tumbling down there? We didn't like the fate of that life size log. But the canoe was bigger and sure to float. (Don't ask.) Might be safest to stay with the canoe.

There was a 12 foot rope attached to the bow, and an identical one tied to the stern. Maybe the best way to be sure we stayed with the boat was for each of us to tie one of those ropes around his waist. That way, if we got thrown out and pulled under, we could grab the rope and pull ourselves back to the canoe on the surface. (Don't ask.)

Well, there's no explaining it with white man's logic. Yes, the ropes could've gotten wrapped around our legs or arms or necks. Yes, the ropes could've gotten wrapped around a tumbling canoe. Yes, it could've been a combination of all of that and worse.

The sun was shining. We were straight and sober. We were healthy, bright, young college men. We were taking our time, studying the situation and thinking it through. We went and got the boat and carried it back to where we'd put in.

With Kip in the bow and me in the stern we each reached for a rope before we shoved off. After we tied the ropes around our waists, we each had about eight feet of slack line lying at our feet. As we aimed for what we thought was the right spot, we had the good sense to feel the trepidation. But that's about all the good sense we had. The current was hurrying the canoe to the dam. We paddled hard to get the momentum we thought we'd need … and besides, maybe if we went fast enough, even if we screwed up, we could get through the whole experience before Murphy's law and nature's other laws could catch up with us.

There was no turning back. All we could do was keep going toward the roar and the bottom we couldn't see except for some wild high splashes jumping higher than the dam. Some last split second corrections to line us up with the flow and over the top we went. We dropped very fast, except for my heart which wound up in my throat.

I remember we got soaked by the spray and water poured into the boat in a huge moment and then we were squirted free, out on flat water amid the little dimpled whirlpools and the downstream drifting bubbles in our upright canoe on a sunny afternoon.

Just that quickly we again looked like a couple of nonchalant college kids out for a gentle paddle on a sunny summer day. Kids, don't try this on your dam at home. But if you do, secure yourself to a life jacket, not to a rope and a boat.

Lean and Teen

Maybe we've been self destructive
but we were life affirming
we've been teasing and pushing
and celebrating
the laws of nature all along
poking under the tent
swinging over the water
we were youthful
we were pissed
at broken rules that wouldn't bend
we were full of belly laughs and vinegar
some vague seventh sense of discipline
saved us from an early grave but
we surely were well wounded.

The World's Farthest North Parking Meters

I can safely tell this story because the statute of limitations has run. In the winter of 1971 I was living in Fairbanks with my old friend Tony Bagnastio (an alias). I'll just describe him by telling how, as a Teamster, he was wild looking and driving big trucks in Alaska as the oil pipeline was being built. One day he pulled into the pipe yard to gas up and some redneck driver who didn't know him growled something unpleasant about Tony being a hippie. Another redneck driver who did know him simply said, "That ain't no hippie - that's a wild man."

Anyway, Tony was living above a car window repair shop in what was essentially the insulated attic of a big garage. I was living alone in a hundred year old log cabin by the power plant about half a mile away burning lumps of coal in a pot bellied stove. But I liked hanging out at Tony's. He had a wood stove and was able to stay warm at 50 below because the shop below was heated and thus he had a warm floor.

We didn't have much to do but smoke, drink, read and rant, so we got pretty good at all of it. A local dicey issue in the newspaper concerned the mayor's controversial decision (before freeze up) to install parking meters in sort of a park area along the river on the north edge of downtown. Some nice old couple had donated that property to the city with the understanding it could be kept an open public space.

The Mayor, Julian Rice (who Tony described as being

as tall laying down as he was standing up), went against the old couple's wishes, paved much of the property and installed what I believe were, in fact, the world's farthest north parking meters.

Late one cold night, Tony and I got to talking about those parking meters, and how lots of folks didn't like either how they got there or the fact that they were there at all. There was an ice fog, it was around two in the morning and about 30 below as I recall. As it happened, the axe we used to chop firewood had a history. It had been brought up to Alaska late in the 19th Century by a storied character and somehow Tony came into possession of it. He held it in high esteem because of its age, its high quality and the stories associated with its original owner from a previous century. I still have that axe today and use it as my main axe every winter, though the handle's been replaced a few times.

Back to the night in question. We were feeling no pain other than the shared pain of everyone in Fairbanks who had to live with those god damn parking meters. Up till that night, the good citizenry had concluded with resignation that the Mayor had spoken and the battle was lost. We decided the situation wasn't that hopeless, that the people were on the high ground on this one and that we could step up to the plate and knock the indignity out of the park.

As you might imagine, the downtown streets were silent and deserted in the middle of the night in an ice fog at around 30 below. We had the area pretty much to ourselves and could work uninterrupted until each and every one of those parking meters was chopped down with a 19th Century axe that had seen more life than the Mayor ever dreamed of.

Actually, we didn't really chop them down. We hit them squarely in the head with the full force of the blunt end of the axe. We decapitated them. It's amazing how super-chilled parking meters explode when struck hard. As if they were wound too tight, pieces went flying into the air glistening in the street lights like the ice fog.

According to the story in the Fairbanks Daily Miner, "Police are looking for those responsible." Tony read that and said, "Of course they haven't caught the culprits, says right here they're looking for people who are 'responsible'." I can tell you for sure that, to this day, they haven't caught those vigilante street theater hooligans.

Wanta fight

Some of my favorite evidence
is circumstantial.

Some of my best ethics
are situational.

Some of my dear teachers
are dead.

Wanta fight?

For the Halibut

In the spring of '73 when I was at Oregon State University in Corvallis trying unsuccessfully to pursue a degree in Landscape Architecture, I got a message from my old friend, alias Tony Bagnastio. He was living on a parcel of land he'd acquired on Chichigoff Island, the outermost island in that part of the Alaskan coastal passage. 90 miles west of Juneau, Tony's place was a short boat ride from the little village of Elfin Cove. When I say "Tony's place," I mean a wooden tent platform built off the ground a foot or so and a big floorless canvas wall tent set upon it. It was probably 12'x16' - pretty good sized.

Tony was urging me to come up and join him for the halibut fishing season in these prime fishing grounds. So when the semester ended I made my way by road up to Juneau, parked my rig and flew out to Elfin Cove on a mail plane that went once or twice a week.

Tony was all excited. He'd restored this classic 15' heavy wood boat, painted eyes on it, and outfitted it with a new seven horsepower Merc and two full skates worth of halibut gear, complete with coiling tubs. It was all high-end gear, and this old boat, though only 15' long, took five shoulders to carry down the hill to the water. I questioned the size of the boat and motor for these waters and Tony launched off into one of his then favorite stories about Charlie Ferdeen who 50 years ago rowed all the way up from Seattle in a boat like this and he did it standing up facing forward. What could go wrong?

At his place ... let's call it a camp, I noticed a separate

tent down the hill and a hefty clothesline holding an open sleeping bag and a pillow. I asked him who lived there and he said she just left on the plane before mine. Turns out she was a rather attractive girl from Seattle.

A fisherman with a small trawler had made his way down to Seattle and met her on the docks. Apparently, they were each looking for a bit of a sea change and he hired her on as his crew. (That size boat doesn't really need a second person, but hey... it can be both helpful and nice.) They made their way back up the coast and for reasons unspecified he left her on the docks in Elfin Cove.

His leaving her might've had something to do with a rather unique circumstance. As it turns out, this young lady, in addition to being fine to look at, exuded a smell most unique. It was a lusty, musty, come hither odor of a circus of hormones, and irrepressible. It was, even to salty old fishermen, overpowering "to the Nth degree."

Well, Elfin Cove is a really rather small and narrow-minded community of people Tony still calls "cove okies." They didn't like this seductress in their midst, especially perhaps the wives. They wanted her gone. Someone concocted a story, maybe they all even came to believe it, about her peeping into someone's window. Fuel to the sexually threatened fires. No one would ever take her in and, in some twisted scary manifestation of collective thinking, the whole village against her, they called the State Troopers back on the mainland and filed a complaint by phone.

She, of course, had no money and nowhere to go. Elfin Cove has a pier for docking boats, a part time post office, a small store and a small café all strung along a boardwalk on the bay. There was no hotel.

Enter Tony. Naturally empathetic to such a plight, he offered her a place to stay. Very quickly he determined he was going to have to set up a separate tent for her out in the breezes . . . so she could have some well deserved peace and privacy.

The Trooper arrived on the next plane. Folks said they figured she must be staying over at Tony's, which was accessible only by boat. The Trooper borrowed a boat and was met at the shore by Tony. An argument ensued in which Tony insisted on a search warrant which the Trooper didn't have. In the middle of it, old Charlie Ferdeen, who was about 90 by then, came out of the woods and listened for awhile. The old man was quite a presence, and eventually he looked the Trooper in the eye with a squint and said, "What're you, some kind of lawman?" The Trooper got back in his borrowed boat and caught the plane before it left.

By the time I got there she was gone on the earlier mail plane, but the little tent was still up with the doors open and the sleeping bag he'd provided was hanging, along with the pillow, on the clothesline in the deep lush forest. I never did go down there to get a whiff.

One other story about strangers. Even though the Elfin Cove locals were suspicious of Tony and, therefore, of me when I arrived, they knew we were fishermen so at some level they accepted us. The same could not be said about a fairly large cabined boat that showed up and tied up to the community dock for a couple of weeks. The boat had four young people on it, two men and two women all pretty much colorful and dishevelled and with no discernable purpose. That in itself was bad enough, but the kicker that alienated pretty much everyone in Elfin Cove was that on the stern of this boat in large professional lettering was the name of the boat – The Quivering Thigh. Even though Tony and I were fishing damn near suicidally, they all knew about Charlie Ferdeen and, compared to the Quivering Thigh, we had credibility... maybe sea cred.

As we got our gear organized and waited for the halibut season to open, one day boating around, we stopped at a secluded shore to have lunch. There were craters in the earth 2-1/2' deep and the same across. They were fresh holes with bits of edge dirt still sloughing in the moist midday sun. "What's that, Tony?" "Bears man. Skunk cabbage. They love skunk cabbage. Pull out the whole goddamn plant at once." Thus ended my comfort level, especially after he told me about the bear he'd seen near our canvas camp.

Eventually we got to fishing. I think I've had over 30 jobs in my life, but this was the hardest work I have ever done. Turns out there are up to 13' tides that move through there to the mainland and back twice a day. That's a helluva lot of water racing through these channels between islands. Setting halibut skates in this environment is tricky but doable, primarily because gravity is on your side. Pulling up those skates is way harder precisely because gravity is pulling the other way, and the tides are going sideways.

We tried to time our skate setting and skate pulling to be between tide floods. But there's only so much one can do in that vast wild world. Let me just say that sometimes, trying unsuccessfully to pull up a skate by hand ("you'll love it, it's the old fashioned way"), we'd tie the buoy rope off on the bow, set full throttle on the motor, head out to sea with the tied rope singing tautly past both of us, engine screaming and we leaning away with one hand over our faces and the other over our nuts.

Let's talk about the whirlpools. Sometimes, when circumstances were just right and the tides were moving, there would be whirlpools out in the middle between island passages that were over a hundred feet in diameter. These are eerie, dangerous things. Lots of local stories of big boats being sucked in and disappearing forever. Well, we had a 15' boat with a seven horse outboard, but had to go through those same passages.

I'm here to tell you that after a long day of pulling

your guts out trying to retrieve your 1800' skate with anchors and who knows how many fish on each of a hundred baited hooks on each skate, including some hefty halibut, all done with tide currents going one way or another, well, it would fine tune your instincts to be coming around these points in the dark with a loaded boat keeping your eyes peeled for giant circles of eerily smooth water that would taper conically down to a center sucking point that had to be several feet lower than the rest of the waving sea. That's how powerful those whirlpools were, and that's how sharp your attention had to be to survive.

That summer we fished every day of the halibut season that it was possible to get our boat out on the water, and a few days we shouldn't have tried. But we never lost our gear, we ate well, we didn't get hurt, we sold our fish to the fish tender ships anchored in the area, and when it was over we had made almost exactly enough money to cover the costs of the boat and the gear.

Brother Tony

Hard edged compassion
might be friendly, might not
walks right up to anything
like he holds the next card.

A most poetic life
simply eclectic
wielding Manjusri's sword
in the bliss of creation
he cuts the crap
with laughter and work
and twin boys.

A music man any old time
a man not to be crossed

You should Write that Down

You can show up someplace new
and Tony will have just left.

The fruit of seasoned nimbleness.

'To live outside the law you must be honest'
as an early hero said
greed and ignorance do not amuse him.

An adroit and capable man
who takes the time to know
both tenderness and survival
A sure footed dynamo
Tony's paid the piper
and he's danced.

Meeting with The Dalai Lama

SETTING THE STAGE

I'd been to Africa twice and overland from Europe to India and back, and spent a winter in Japan studying their religious traditions and landscaping styles. So an invitation to join a round-the-world year-long trip to study some of the world's great religions was a welcome opportunity for more adventurous travel with a spiritual focus in the company of the leading communicator of the world's religions in the English speaking world – the one and only Huston Smith, a truly remarkable man.

It was an academic year sponsored by the International School of America (run by a lovely man from Bath, England). It was technically run through Harvard, but my way in was through Syracuse University - part of my Master's Degree work I was fortunate to get into through my main professor, my mentor, Huston. He was leading a team of three professors, including himself, Victor Danner (U. of Indiana) and Robert Gross (Berkeley/Minnesota) and their families. There were about 25 students from the U.S. and Canada.

ADVICE FROM AN ALCHEMIST ALONG THE WAY

We started in England, spent a month in Morocco and two weeks in Israel and settled in for a month in Iran. Iran is a wild and beautiful country of contrasts, rich in history, art and intrigue.

My travels had (and have) been rich and rewarding. Every place I learned. Wouldn't trade my experience for the world ... because that's what it was. But those travels had from time to time (more times than I'd like) given me intestinal problems that had sometimes weakened me and often lingered.

One day in Isfahan, we had the opportunity to meet with a traditional Persian alchemist. (I surely wish I could remember his name.) He too was a remarkable man. He was solid, elfish, pragmatic, out there, engaged, ageless, healthy looking. As I recall he took us into an underground room where, surrounded by jars and equipment, he answered questions.

I had some time to consider what I might ask him. (It's amazing what one thinks of.) I asked something like this: "Sometimes when you're traveling to far distant places, you get sick. Bad guts. It makes it harder to get a jazzed first impression of a place. Is there anything one can do to minimize that?"

My colleagues chuckled. The old alchemist smiled. He told me that before I begin a trip to faraway places, I should collect some dirt from my home area. (This was all being translated.) He said to make sure it was good, clean dirt. The alchemist said to take some with me. And every time I move to a much different area, I should take (eat/drink) some of the dirt. He said it would help to keep stable the flora and fauna of my intestinal tract. I asked him how much of a dose to take. We eventually understood each other at about a teaspoon full.

Well, it was too late to do anything about that trip. But I remembered what the old alchemist said the next trip when I went to Thailand, India, Ladakh, Sikkim, Nepal, Hong Kong, Taiwan, Japan and Alaska. That trip was a full year with a lot of bad water and biospheric changes. Before my wife and I started that journey, I gathered up some clean dirt from around our home in North Dakota. I put it in a plastic bag and hoped for the best at all the customs posts. This was in 1980 and '81 and the bag of dirt never created a problem at customs. Each place we went, either on the way there or just after we arrived, I took a spoonful of dirt. I scooped it out of the bag and stirred it into tea or coffee – let it cool a little and as I recall drank it fairly fast.

On that year-long, low-budget, multi-country trip, I had far less trouble with my guts than I ever had before. My wife is a fine traveling companion, but though she was curious, she didn't like swallowing dirt and grimaced at my spoonfuls. I shall conclude politely by affirming that her intestinal circumstances required much more frequent accommodation than mine during the course of that trip.

HUSTON'S BOOK AS A CALLING CARD

After a rich month studying Islam and Persian culture, including the rare opportunity of living in a Sufi Khaniqah, we went to India. Having been there before, being intrigued by the Tibetans and needing a little space, I went off from the group to the Himalayan foothills to a little town called McLeod Gunj (from the British Raj days), in and around what is perhaps the heart of the Tibetan exile life. In McLeod Gunj at that time were the Tibetan government's Palace in Exile, the Tibetan School of Medicine, the Library of Tibetan Works and Archives, the Tibetan Handicraft Center (run by the Dalai Lama's sister), monasteries, shrines, iconographic stone carvers, illicit home brew (chang) shops, a few foreigners, and some spartan hotels and cafes. It was (and hopefully still is) a wonderful Himalayan hillside community alive with positive energy.

I knew that Huston Smith and the Dalai Lama were friends and had been for many years by then. I was traveling with a copy of Huston's most recent book called, "Forgotten Truth: The Primordial Tradition", a wonderful book addressing the core themes of most all spiritual traditions in a very accessible way – it even has diagrams! I was in McLeod Gunj for a few weeks to write a paper about Tibetan Buddhism. Seemed like a good idea to figure out how to get a copy of Huston's new book to the Dalai Lama, since I was in town anyway.

Through a series of inquiries I learned that the Dalai Lama's Personal Secretary, Tenzin Geshe, walked through a particular little park most days at noon. I knew that he was a monk in robes who spoke English. So I walked up to him one noon in the park, told him I was Huston Smith's student and that on behalf of Huston I'd like to give him (the Secretary) a copy of Huston's new book for him to give to the Dalai Lama.

This most gracious man said he too knew of Huston and Huston's friendship with His Holiness and yes indeed he would be sure His Holiness got the book. He paused for just a second and then said he had perhaps a better idea. He said as it turns out His Holiness is in a 90-day retreat, but it's soon over. He said His Holiness will be in Bodhgaya in a month, and if we were going to be around Huston and I could deliver the book in person there and then. I put the book back in my bag, confirmed the date and said I'd be there, hopefully with Huston.

April, McLeod Gunj

One night in a little Himalayan house
in the woods outside McLeod Gunj
there was a spider who busily kept building
and rebuilding a web
between several melting candles.
Finally it rested,
suspended on a few remaining strands.
Oh, I thought, how pitiful
its limited frustrated lowly life
when all of a sudden it hurried off
straight up in the air!

A couple weeks later I rejoined the group, keen to tell Huston what had been done. He, of course, was overjoyed, but with deep regret felt he must decline this most unique opportunity because of his commitment to this traveling school which, by the date of the proposed meeting, would be nowhere near Bodhgaya.

This was cause for thought. I just couldn't justify hoarding this unexpected and truly unique opportunity for myself. Seemed to me the only thing worse would've been showing up with a big group. So I invited three people who were on this trip: Huston's wife, Kendra, his protégé, Phil Novak, and a friend, Crystal Woodward. Yes, of course, they said yes, of course.

On the appointed day we showed up at the Tibetan Temple in Bodhgaya. Bodhgaya was at that time literally a one-elephant town in the hot dusty plains of India in the state of Bihar. But Bodhgaya is unique in history and fact. I won't get into it here, but you'll remember the story of the guy who became known as Buddha who, 2500 years ago, with a determined mind, sat under a tree and attained enlightenment. Well, that tree was in Bodhgaya. In fact, the descendant of that tree is still growing there, large and healthy and adjacent to a temple.

Every (or nearly so) Asian country with a significant Buddhist population has a temple compound in Bodhgaya. It's the site of pilgrimages and meditation retreats. The Tibetans, of course, have a fine Tibetan place there.

A MOST MEMORABLE MORNING

So we showed up. The Dalai Lama's Personal Secretary, Tenzin Geshe, remembered me and said it would be fine if in Huston's stead I brought his wife and two more. We were instructed in some basic Tibetan protocols pertaining to greeting the Dalai Lama: prayer scarf offered, blessed and returned, bows with hands clasped (which were reciprocated, of course).

Soon we were ushered into a very Tibetan room with His Holiness sitting on cushions on the floor behind a low table. He stood up with a big beaming smile to greet us then sat back down after asking us to sit first, also on cushions around the low table. His Secretary sat at one end. He was pleased to receive Huston's book.

After pleasantries and inquiries as to Huston, His Holiness asked if there was anything we'd like to ask him. He didn't have to do that. We would've been well pleased to have been ushered out at that point having presented our gift and received his blessing. I don't know that I've ever met a more genuine, thoughtful, compassionate person. He's one of the singularly best educated people in the history of the world; well versed in religion, history, science, psychology, spiritual practice, world politics, you name it. But at the same time very unassuming and with the openness of a child.

There's a line in the important documentary Huston did of Tibetan Buddhism years earlier called "Requiem for a Faith." It occurs in the context of a description of the formal dialectical arguments that are part of the practice of some Tibetan monks. In fact, there's a sight to be seen in McLeod Gunj that still makes me smile. As you walk along a wide path on the outskirts of town there up on the hillside is a building with two large open windows. And there you might see two monks, one visible in each window, playing ping pong right above the sign that says, "Tibetan School of Dialectics." Cracked me up every time.

Anyway, in "Requiem for a Faith" in describing this monastic training in dialectics they show two monks debating in a formal yet artistic way. One is asking the other something like, "If indeed there is no soul, what transmigrates?" This refers to the Buddhist understanding that there is no permanent "I", and yet at the same time there is reincarnation. In the film the question is never answered. So we asked the Dalai Lama.

I probably shouldn't try to recreate His Holiness's answer to a question posed in a private audience more than 30 years ago, but I'm going to venture a short paraphrase to this question and then a longer answer to another question as well . . . I don't think he'd mind.

At that time the Dalai Lama was less sure of his English than he is now, and most of this private audience was happening through Tenzin Geshe acting as translator. But it was funny, sometimes when the Secretary was offering us a translation of what His Holiness was saying His Holiness would interrupt the translator and correct him with his own preferred word or phrase. It was slightly comical and most intriguing.

So in answering the question "if indeed there is no soul, what transmigrates?" His Holiness said that regrettably the English language was not well equipped for the subtleties of things spiritual. It is a logical language that excels in some areas of expression, but is unfortunately lacking as a spiritual language. He said that as he currently understood English the closest proximation of a term to answer the question was the English word "light ... clear light."

My biggest, most personal question was long, and he gave it his full attention. I told him that the most important thing in life to me was the unfolding of wisdom. What I wanted most out of life was to understand as much as possible, as deeply as possible. Therefore, with that as my primary and abiding interest, was it a mistake to live an active life in modern western society?

He said no, not necessarily. Wisdom can be found and cultivated anywhere. He said that if it was by definition a hindrance to live in the West then he wouldn't be sending his monks to Europe and the States! And with that he laughed a bit.

I pressed on. I said I came from a rural, agricultural region and had the opportunity to become a farmer if I chose. Would such a livelihood be a distraction or hindrance to the unfoldment and cultivation of wisdom?

He said no, not necessarily. He described how in Tibet the monks and monasteries were very active in agriculture over the centuries, no innate obstacles there. However, he went on to caution, if one is truly serious about the spiritual development of wisdom, it is a good idea to not raise animals with the intention of killing them, even for food. He said to do so could put a bit of a dark karmic cloud over your place and your main endeavors of spiritual unfoldment.

He went on to explain that intention was the key. He said the monks in these vast agricultural monasteries in Tibet plowed the ground regularly to plant the barley. Now it is true that as the plow moves through the ground no doubt some small beings die by that act. But that is not the monk's intention. His intention is to plant the barley. He noted that the eating of meat that others have killed does not carry that same karmic baggage (that's my phrase, I don't remember his). Similarly, when you're driving down the road in a car to get from point A to point B, no doubt some bugs or other small beings will be hit by the car and die. But since their death is not your intention, you are not adversely affecting your karma or your spiritual unfoldment.

His Holiness's degree of engagement in this American stranger's questions was remarkable to me. There was no formality, no hurry, and no sense of perfunctory politeness. He and I were talking about the same thing, with mutual interest in the subject matter and taking the time it took to address the issues.

Our conversation went on until it had run its course

and we felt we needed to allow him to move on to the many other things he no doubt was being counted on to do.

There was a Tibetan protocol of respect that we followed, perhaps clumsily, in making our departure, but His Holiness was jovial, serious, patient and kind throughout. One of the most memorable mornings of my life. The kind that leaves a visual memory and sticks with you.

Finding Right Livelihood

This will not likely appear in an anthology of career planning tips.

After five different majors spread over eight off-and-on years, I got a BA in World Religions which led to an MA/PhD scholarship. But by the time I finished the MA, I'd had enough of academia and couldn't see what I'd do with a PhD in religion anyway.

About that time I got an offer from my dad to come home and join my brother in slowly taking over the family business which centered around farm land (management, appraisal, sales). I saw a taoistic simplicity which appealed to me, so I moved home to do it. It was the worst job I ever had. The nature of the work, as it turned out, didn't suit my nature, and I didn't like working with my relatives.

By this time I was married, 28 and had not ever worked for a year straight through at anything. I returned to some skills I'd acquired working in Alaska in the late 60's and early 70's and took a job as a land surveyor building roads. "Paving the Way" I liked to call it (still looking for that taoistic simplicity). I still couldn't see the future career-wise, but North Dakota and our circumstances there didn't feel like where we ought to be at the time. We had other interests. So we saved up some money and took off to India for a year for reasons described in my story called "Tenzin's Name."

A friend of ours was in law school at UND at the time and persuaded me that a law degree could be a versatile credential. So I picked up an application and stuck it in my bag as we packed for India. Didn't get around to filling it out till we were in a hotel in Bangkok. I pulled it out and noticed it said it had to be typed. The hotel didn't have a typewriter, so I noted that on the top of the first page and filled it out longhand. I think it was the desire to travel light as much as anything else that caused me to invest in a stamp and an envelope and get that paper out of my backpack before we left for Ladakh.

Nearly a year later we returned to the States and contemplated a career in landscaping in Oregon as we made our way to our pile of mail back in North Dakota. In that mail was a letter from the law school saying congratulations, school starts in a week. I did the only thing I could think of - took Krista and a good friend and a boat and went fishing for a few days at my favorite lake in Canada, trying to decide what to do. By the time we took the boat out of the water I was persuaded to go to law school, primarily because it put off getting a real job for another three years – and I was somewhat intrigued by the notion of the versatility of the lawyer credential.

A million things to do on Monday
But nothing really for the rest of my life.

So it was back to school. I was 34 when I was finishing my last year of law school, and Krista and I talked about what to do next. It was agreed that I was so bad at chemistry and the hard sciences that med school was out of the question, and I would be forced to get a job. We've always respected the traditional Buddhist teachings called the Noble Eightfold Path, and particularly in this context the one called "Right Livelihood," which counsels that finding good work of benefit to others benefits oneself as well. Well, aware of the versatility of the law credential, we thought broadly about what we would most like to do. Those deliberations and imaginings resulted in what I thought was a rather impressive resumé and cover letter ... and a who's-who-type address list of some of our favorite international organizations (Greenpeace, Amnesty International, some of the population control organizations, etc.). The cover letter described our extensive third world travel backgrounds, a commitment to justice, our professional skills (Krista was a Med Tech at the time) and our offer to devote a decade of our lives to the work of that organization, including a willingness to live anywhere in the world that their work might take us. We made it clear that we had few outside obligations other than school loan debts, and that we could work for their low nonprofit wages. I remember the heady feeling on the day I carried those letters (there were a couple dozen organizations we sent them to) down to the post office and turned them loose. I felt like I was making a big offer to some lucky group, and had a sense of wonder about casting my fate to the winds on that day.

I should also mention that in addition to the well known organizations we had selected to send the resumé to, there was one other that I hadn't heard of before. I was the Student Director of the Legal Aid Clinic at my law school at the time, and one day walking down the hall in the law school basement (where it seems all legal aid clinics reside), I noticed a little job posting describing an Indian legal aid attorney position on a reservation in Nebraska. The description said it was for a single Indian law attorney office that would serve three Indian reservations from a town of 940 people on one of the reservations. Well, I thought what the hell, I already have the resumé written, might as well simplify the cover letter and get another envelope and stamp. So I did, and then more or less forgot about having sent it.

Graduation was approaching and I was hurrying home every day looking for mail from all my favorite organizations. It started to trickle in. In the end I think only half of those groups even responded. Of those that did, none offered me a job, or any encouragement or advice. Some of them (I won't say which ones) even sent cold letters that said something like, 'sorry, we don't have any openings, but please find enclosed our donation materials, we would appreciate it if you could make a substantial financial contribution to our work, and thank you in advance.' I was so pissed off and disappointed I didn't send any of them anything for years.

Then one day a letter arrived from the Legal Aid Society in Omaha, Nebraska, which said essentially, "how soon can you get here for an interview?"

I got the job, and before packing to move to the reservation I told my dad about having found work. The conversation went like this:

> James: *Well, Dad, I got a job.*
> Vernon: *As a lawyer?*
> James: *Yup.*
> Vernon: *Never thought I'd see the day. What kind of law practice is it?*
> James: *I'm going to be doing Indian rights work. Helping tribes and their members protect and use their rights as Indians.*
> Vernon: *Well, I hope they pay you well and I hope you lose.*

I didn't tell him that the job paid just $15,000 a year, plus a $600 a year bonus for remote duty pay for the first three years. After that, no bonus. They figured if you were still there then it was because you wanted to be.

Several years later, over a scotch, I reminded my father of that conversation. Then I said, "Well Dad, it didn't really work out that way. I don't get paid worth a damn, but we're really kickin' ass."

We had seven wonderful years living and working on those Nebraska Indian reservations, starting with when I first arrived and went to see the highly respected Winnebago Tribal Chairman, Reuben Snake (the subject of another story), who extended his hand, gave me a big smile and said, "I've been waiting for you."

It's now been over 25 years practicing exclusively in the area of Indian law, always for a nonprofit law firm, the first for those seven years, and since then 20 and counting with the second firm in Wisconsin. I've long since forgiven those prestigious organizations we offered a decade of our lives to and who asked instead for cash. We even send them a little money once in a while.

Hooky

Long into the blue afternoon
of September
the grass yet green yet
maples more shades
of red than we'll ever name.

Snapping turtle tail trails
slip into the water
a warm and welcome southern breeze
lets the migrators stop and eat
some of them sing right into my ears.

To build a fire
is the question of the hour
on this long blue hooky day
there is no progress here
all is well.

Tenzin's Name

Krista and I both came of age in the '60's. We met at age 28 and married at 29. It was a first for both of us. By that time we each had been around the block and had a pretty good idea of who we were. In comparing our pasts, we discovered that neither of us had a close personal friend whose first marriage had lasted. We were confident enough in our love that this fact did not dissuade us from getting married, but it did give us pause about bringing children into the world.

Since neither of us had a career at that time or any real commitments other than to each other, we came up with a rather unique and wonderful plan that turned out very well. We had each been to India in earlier years (me twice) and each had found that India deepened the soul, raised the spirit, and profoundly challenged world views and relationships. So we decided to go there for a year, on a lean budget, and if we still wanted to make babies together after that there was a good chance it would work. So we did.

We had day jobs. I as a surveyor for a road construction company, Krista as a Med. Tech. in a Human Nutrition lab. And, with my father as a cosigner, we bought a smoke damaged house in Grand Forks which we lived in and fixed up. After a year, we sold the house and took off for the East for a year.

During that year we were in Thailand, India, Ladakh, Sikkim, Nepal, Hong Kong, Taiwan and Japan. But most of the year we spent in the Himalayas (India, Ladakh, Sikkim,

Nepal) where the name Tenzin is as common as John is over here. We met a lot of cool Tenzins and read about a few more.

About nine months after we returned to the States we were living in a farm house near Grand Forks. I'd just finished my first year of law school and Krista was eight and a half months pregnant. I went fishing alone in Minnesota for a few days. One evening while I was cooking up some fish there was a knock on the cabin door. It was some friends of the family who'd tracked me down to tell me Krista was unexpectedly in labor.

I threw everything in my old pick-up and headed home, but it took awhile. First the truck died at a traffic light in Bemidji. I persuaded a State Trooper to give me a ride halfway to North Dakota, and my brother, John, to come from Grand Forks and meet us there. It worked out (except for the speeding ticket my brother got on the way which I should've paid for but don't think I ever did).

I got back to the farm late in the night in time to wash new diapers in the wringer washer and wait for the ambulance. Krista had been in labor all day. It was supposed to be a home birth and she had a midwife and a friend there. But the baby was lodged face forward and just wouldn't come out. He was born in the hospital early the next morning. And he was born without a name.

We'd been exploring names for months, but couldn't quite settle on anything. The birth forced the issue. One of the difficulties in selecting a name came from the fact that neither Krista nor I are Christian and we didn't want to saddle the kid with a name that had Christian religious roots or connotations.

The more we talked about it the more we kept coming back to all those good thoughts and feelings we had around the name Tenzin. And just five short days after he was born he became Tenzin August (the middle name in honor of my vitally important great grandfather).

I remember going to my father and a conversation that went very much like this:

> James: *Well, Dad, we have a name for your first grandchild.*
> Vernon: *Good. What is it?*
> James: *Tenzin.*
> Vernon: (Staring straight ahead with no discernable expression.) *Well, I guess that's better than Ninezin or Elevenzin.*

Babies and little kids are not where my interests naturally go. Fortunately, Krista is Mother Nurture for babies and infants. But, of course, when the kid is yours you tend to pay some attention. For instance, if I wanted a little candle-lit private time with Krista I'd open the pots and pans cupboard and pull them about half way out. Then I'd plunk Tenzin down in the middle of it, give him a couple of wooden spoons and sneak away for awhile.

Then finally one day when he was three I said to him, "Put on your shoes and get in the car," and damn if he didn't actually do it! I was speechless for a moment, then looked at Krista and said, "Hey, this might work out. What's his name again?"

First Child

A child is coming
new light in the world
if it isn't a struggle
I'll make it a struggle.

A child is coming
as a wish coming true
to share our love
in a furthering way

A person coming together
through the flux of change
to be with us awhile
the being has begun

Someone's coming
my lover, my friend
I wait on splendid earth
for something coming true.

As a child one comes asking
we will be here
someone is coming
the being has begun.

Getting to Katelin

At the end of summer in '86, we were living on our $50 a month farmstead on the Omaha Indian Reservation. Tenzin was four and becoming a lot of fun for me. Krista had a year or two earlier told me she'd gone through premature menopause, which meant among other things we wouldn't be making any more babies. So we'd long since discontinued any precautions in that regard.

Coincidentally, Krista had given away most all of Tenzin's baby clothes and things just three weeks prior to this story.

We were flat broke. All our money was in a thin checking account, and most of our free time was spent at home or close to it. So when I got a chance to go to Boulder for a meeting and a long weekend with most expenses paid, I jumped at it. The Native American Rights Fund was hosting some late week meetings on Indian rights issues that I was involved with. My dear friend and co-counsel Bob Peregoy, who worked at NARF, offered me his spare bedroom and we planned on doing some good goofing off on the weekend.

It was about a nine hour drive to Boulder, but the weather and the road were good and I got there and participated in the meetings till they ended Friday afternoon. It was time to kick back and hang out with Bob, which I'd been looking forward to for weeks.

But somehow late Friday night I started thinking of Krista in a longing sort of way. It was a peculiar and very unexpected feeling. I mean we were together a lot, and this was a rare chance for a mini-vacation, boys' weekend with a good old friend – nothing pressing back at home. But this feeling persisted and grew in the pit of my stomach; it was a feeling of love and attraction.

Saturday morning I woke up and started packing my bag. Bob woke up and asked what I was doing. I said I wasn't really sure why, but I was just compelled to go home. Felt bad about missing the rest of the weekend together, and it was nothing personal toward Bob, but I just needed to get home to Krista. Bob fixed me a good breakfast and I took off.

I got past Denver and out on the open highway headed east. Sometimes when I get in just the right lonely space I get a desire to write. This was one of those times. I didn't have anything particular in mind to write, but I just like to respond to the muse when the urge arrives. It's a good idea to be responsive to that and just drop everything and see what comes out. An idea started to take shape, it was just a simple notion to write something to another old friend, Steve Stolee, an artistically talented guy I'd grown up with but hadn't seen for some years. I had no idea what he was doing at the time, but somehow felt compelled to tell him what I was doing at that exact moment.

This notion of communicating something to Steve Stolee was taking shape and I was getting in the zone. I was rolling along at about 75 mph on the interstate with a good pen in my pocket but I had a problem. My writing pad was in a corner of the back seat out of reach. I didn't want to pull over. The road was in a drone and my head was in the zone. There was a flow of momentum.

So I figured if I left the cruise control on and planned my moves just right I could let go of the wheel, turn and reach and retrieve my tablet and be back sitting down facing forward hands on the wheel in about two seconds, maybe three. I rehearsed it and went for it. I'm still not sure what happened, maybe I bumped the steering wheel with my knee. Anyway, things started happening pretty fast right about then.

I did manage to grab the writing tablet, but by the time I was back in my seat behind the wheel the car was veering crazily all over both eastbound lanes. It was swerving from one shoulder to the other and I remember it rocking so much in the process I thought it was going to roll. It was damn close to a disaster, maybe a fatal one since in order to get to the paper I'd taken my seat belt off. Fortunately, I'd chosen my moment carefully and there were no other cars real close by. But I remember the cars in the westbound lanes slowing down and pulling over to their far right shoulder. It took a number of very long slow motion seconds for me to regain control of the car, but somehow I did. Needless to say by that point the feng shui of the drone and the zone had been radically disrupted. But I pulled it back together (without stopping) and went on to write the following poem at 73 mph:

For Stolee's Mail

I'm in eastern Colorado
doin' 73 mph
driving into the morning sun headed home
out here where the nation's breasts are named
Country and Western
and water has no rights
motoring home from a Denver meeting
enjoying a stone alone
dreaming of my children
and the sacred nature of nature
9 miles from Ovid
rolling plains and bad policies everywhere
a nice home and a few trees
are worth their weight in gold

Johnnie has expensive toys
Donovan has a job
Fred became a doctor
and Micklin just disappeared
Maybe Dukakis can beat Bush
but we need better government
than we deserve
since people have piles of paper
claiming they own the earth
you'd think they'd
dummy up and give a shit
sometimes America seems like an ignoble experiment
Earth as butt wipe
for a diarrhetic ass
and sometimes I am light with awe
Anyway Stephen
it's hours later going past
"original pony express station"
south Nebraska
I just turned down an Indian law position at U.N.D.
heading back to the Rez
it's late July, nearly pow-wow time
I want to go fishing with my beautiful son
there will be other moves
it's easier for me to believe in
what I do for a living
than it is to go fishing
or pay the rent
The highway is full of characters
just like history
rock crushers and skin heads
billboard gluers and tree surgeons
new friends and influenced people
movers, shakers, and sleeping beauties
white beards, white glasses
all kinds of badges on all kinds of sleeves
people happy to be alive and dead ducks

lovers bouncing along in trucks
people who talk nasty
there's a fellow in the other lane
one hand on the wheel and one on his brain
mirrors on his rain soaked windows
dark-eyed desperados slinking home sad-eyed
senators racing away
horse's tail in a trailer door
horse's ass in the slow lane
vintage footage from America on Parade
what's this fellow thinking
sneaking up behind
with a lady in his lap
must be going as fast as he can
road builders, body builders
rock'n roll buses in a row
the highway is full of characters
maybe even someone I know
cops on the beat, hikers on the street
bikers and bankers
at the wayside stopped
some hurried some worried
some faster than stink
stereophonic 3-D road show
the bitch in the station
is looking most glum
the bearded kid by the bridge
has a sunburned thumb
cartoon beaneries and dog fights
muskrat guts and headlights
we got cruise control and self control
and variations on a theme
truck driver looking down a fat lady's dress
making the pass that he knows best
whole families on the riverside
are they planning a future?
maybe just being as they are

the boys in the back of the school bus
are mooning some professor's van
everybody's moving approximately
as fast as they can
salt and pepper sideburns
orange and purple hair
the highway is a theater
gallon of gas the fare
The Platte looks wide and inviting
from a speeding car
old car new car
bird in the sky
miles to go before I die.

Many long hours of solitude later long after dark I pulled into our farmstead lane, still compelled by this overwhelming good feeling of love, went into the house and woke up Krista.

I told her I'd been somehow overwhelmed with love for her and it had catapulted me home. It was one of those precious moments where you leave yourself totally vulnerable confessing a bottomless heart of love. Krista, a woman of vast capacities, heard me just the way I was.

Nine months later Katelin was born in that same bed in that same house. She came out of Krista as a beautiful baby; she came out of me like this:

Katelin Mae Comes with Summer

A full fledgling being
female and fresh
emanates
from one spirit world to another
and is lifted straight to the breast.

A bundle of being, a stage and play

where creation breathes and multiplies
earthshaking, symphonic, pure
she appears as the dance itself
something old doing new.

A HO. May this little baby
> *Katelin Mae come to know*
> *all about her friends*
> *from the power of her mother's milk*
> *to the birds up above in the wind.*

> *May this pretty girl*
> *Katelin Mae come to know*
> *the creatures and their seasons*
> *of stars and books and love*
> *sweet reverence for life.*

> *May this grand lady*
> *Katelin Mae come to know*
her relatives in every kingdom
And may I be with her night and day
to sing her corners smooth.
A HO.

On the night you were born
there was music, cedar and love
Kelly, Kathy, Grandma Gen
your mother and I, and a little bird
perched by the door all night.
Welcome young lady
May your way be deep
And your step light

Winnebago Retrocession

When I first got to the Nebraska Indian reservations in 1984, right out of law school, to be the only "Indian law" attorney in a tiny legal aid office, I went to see the Winnebago Tribe's Chairman, Reuben Alvis Snake, Jr. He gave me a hearty handshake, a smile and said, "I've been waiting for you." He then invited me to sit down because there were a few things we had to do.

Reuben said we had to change the law to stop the state from taking Indians' kids out of their homes and giving them to non-Indian families. He said there should be a state holiday commemorating Little Priest, a great Winnebago leader who died making peace a hundred years ago. Reuben said, most importantly, we needed to get "retrocession" for the Winnebago Tribe.

I was sitting across the table from Reuben, leaning back in my chair (it was a blue jean-to-blue jean meeting) with a legal pad in my lap taking notes. When he said "retrocession" I raised the top of my legal pad a little so he couldn't tell I was writing it out phonetically. I'd never heard the word before (turns out it means to cede back).

Over the next couple weeks I figured it out. In the 1950's the federal government was trying to "get out of the Indian business." It was an era of federal Indian policy that was actually formally called "The Termination Era." I'm talking about the 1950's! Anyway, up to that time, through the Indian treaties and other federal laws, there was a federal/tribal government-to-government relationship. The feds had certain treaty-based responsibilities for the treaty tribes, including public safety which included law enforcement and a court system. In this Termination Era, one of many awful things the feds did to "get out of the Indian business" was to pass a law called Public Law 83-280 (PL-280), in which the feds "gave" to the states the feds' responsibilities regarding criminal and civil jurisdiction. This was an experiment that initially was tried in five states. Unfortunately, Nebraska was one of them.

It's important to know that what the feds "gave" to the state in '53 was the federal portion of jurisdiction. Up till then jurisdiction was shared or "concurrent" between the feds and the Tribe, based on treaty law. It's a fundamental principle of common sense that you can only give away that which is yours. In other words, the Tribe never lost its share of jurisdictional power, it just went dormant when federal support was withdrawn. The problem was that without federal, treaty based support, the Tribe had no resources with which to exercise its jurisdiction. This meant that law enforcement and the courts were only provided by the County.

When PL-280 was passed in '53 and gave the feds' share of concurrent jurisdictional authority to the five states, neither the states nor the tribes were consulted, and none were pleased. To the tribes it was a unilateral encroachment on the nation-to-nation integrity of their treaties; to the states it was an unfunded mandate.

The failed and disgusting "Termination Era" policies of the '50's were repudiated and replaced as part of the civil rights movement of the '60's with a new federal Indian policy which is known as the "Self Determination Policy." Part of that evolution included the enactment of the Indian Civil Rights Act which, among other things, created a mechanism for the tribes to get out from under state jurisdiction and back to a federal/tribal relationship. Unfortunately, the mechanism created required that a tribe persuade the state to ask the feds to take their jurisdiction back.

It should be noted that it's a generally observable fact that the closer one is to an Indian reservation, the more racism there is. In other words, as a general rule flagrant racism diminishes and objectivity increases as you move from county to state to federal government.

So in 1984 the Winnebagos decided to make a push to try to persuade the state of Nebraska to give up its jurisdiction on their reservation. This would put the Tribe back in a preferred government-to-government relationship with the U.S. and restore federal funding to the Tribe for the tribal provision of law enforcement and a tribal court system. They could then govern their own people. Let's talk about what was going on on the ground that made the Winnebagos prioritize this issue.

During the preceding 19 years, law enforcement in Thurston County, Nebraska, was under the control of Sheriff Clyde Storie. From an Indian perspective, it was essentially a reign of terror. Clyde was a barrel-chested, big-gutted redneck who stood about 5'3" in his tight-fitting polyester uniform. At this point in the story, feel free to start thinking about the Napoleon complex.

Clyde had earlier in his reign gone down to the Unicameral (the only single body state legislature in the country) and persuaded them that it was a hugely unfair burden to place on Thurston County taxpayers to provide all this disproportionate law enforcement required to keep "his Indians" in their place. So the state passed a law that said the state would pay the County Sheriff's Office $50 for every day each Indian was in the Thurston County Jail. The law became known as "The Indian Bounty Act" and here comes why.

The good Sheriff employed various family members in his law enforcement enterprise, including his wife who had the food contract. Clyde might've been a world class asshole, but he wasn't entirely an idiot. Didn't take Clyde long to figure out that he could go out in his Sheriff's car after dinner in the evening and head on over to the part of the county where most of the Indians were. He could get all bellicose and belligerent and arrest a couple of them the way only a tight buttoned, red-faced sawed off, mean-assed sheriff could. He'd then haul them over to his County Jail (about 15 miles), book them in (after dinner, remember) and then turn them loose in the predawn hours (before breakfast) and suggest, not very politely, that he didn't really care how or if they got home.

Well, if you do the math, the record will show that each of those Indians was in the jail for two calendar days. That's a hundred bucks an Indian and you don't even have to give them a cup of bad coffee.

Clyde was a piece of work. There were unproved allegations of him raping Indian women in his jail, of him poaching deer with the search light on his Sheriff's car and threatening Indians who caught him in the act that he'd arrest their kids if they didn't keep quiet. The stories were legion and for the most part impossible to prove.

Eventually even the state got disgusted (thanks to the heroic and illustrious Senator Ernie Chambers and others) and repealed the Indian Bounty Act. This, of course, had the effect of really pissing Clyde off and, as one might expect, he blamed the Indians.

Some years after the state took away the bounty money, they did give him (and probably every other county Sheriff) a stun gun. But before we talk about the stun gun, I have to introduce Louie LaRose because he's going to show up in the rest of this story at pretty much every important moment, including with the infamous stun gun.

Louie LaRose is perhaps the most naturally, profoundly funny person I've ever known. He had been the Chairman of the Winnebago Tribe during the civil rights/AIM/Indian Pride/need-new-young leadership days. Unfortunately, those days also happened to be his drinking days and the stories about what he was doing all around the country at intertribal meetings (he told me he was an "all conference Indian") reached home, and to make a very rich and complex and funny story unforgivably short... well, they stopped electing him.

Here's one quick Louie LaRose story. Those big intertribal conferences would be held in the big fancy hotels. Although he enjoys identifying himself as Luke Warmwater, in this circumstance, Louie would make a dinner reservation at the big fancy restaurants under the name Charlie War. Then, when the restaurant receptionist would call out over the loudspeaker that their table was ready, just before Louie (a large man) and his buddies walked in to be seated everyone would hear over the speaker, "War... party of four."

After that, Louie couldn't get elected dog catcher even though he'd sobered up. To hear him tell it he's in "internal exile." Although to be fair, it should be noted that in recent years he's created a tribal buffalo restoration project and served as interim President of the Little Priest Tribal College in Winnebago. In fact, the College got accredited under Louie's watch. But enough about Louie for now, I just wanted to introduce him so you'd be ready as he pops up later.

Let's get back to why the Winnebagos thought they could go down to the Nebraska Unicameral in 1985 and say, "How do you do? We're from the Winnebago Indian Reservation and we'd like you to give up all of your jurisdictional authority over us." Well, to be sure some of the immediacy of it had to do with the notorious Sheriff Clyde Storie. But the story is deeper and I won't do it justice here. Someday a full Winnebago articulation will be written. I'll just say that Reuben Snake was a visionary. He was a practical visionary, which is a rare breed of snake or any other animal. Reuben had a 20-year plan for economic self-sufficiency for the Tribe. In his view, one of the primary, foundational centerpieces of that plan had to be the reassertion of self-control. The Tribe had to be able to make its own laws and be governed by them. Without that capacity for self-determination the resurgence of Winnebago culture was not likely to happen.

So I studied up on PL-280 and retrocession and Reuben called and asked me to come over to the Tribal Office and meet Bob Peregoy, an attorney from the Native American Rights Fund, who wanted to get involved. NARF is to this day the premiere Indian rights legal organization in the country. Bob is from the Flathead Indian Reservation, also in his mid-30's at the time and, like me, fresh out of law school. Fortunately, he had a lot of Indian rights experience prior to going to law school at Berkeley. Bob created the Indian Studies Program at Montana State, and knew his way in political issues.

Bob and I hit it off instantly. He had a wild hair or two and a twinkle in his eye and I just relax into my best work in that environment. It is key to this story to point out that in retrospect the only reason we were able to pull this off was that we were too naïve to realize that it was impossible. So we went ahead and did it, albeit by the skin of our teeth, but I'm getting ahead of my own damn story.

Reuben knew what we were up against, but he really wanted it to happen and he liked the energy and chemistry of Bob and me, so he turned us loose. We worked obsessively on Winnebago retrocession for two years. Fortunately, NARF had a budget, whereas I barely had heat in my office. I did, however, have Sister Tim, the feisty iconoclastic Executive Director of the Legal Aid Society down in Omaha ... she was my boss. Not many nuns, even lay nuns like Tim that you can call iconoclastic. But then again not many nuns that'll flip you the bird if you do something stupid in traffic.

Bob had the institutional clout and resources of NARF, so I bunked with him. There were times when we'd spend one whole week after another camped in a single motel room in Lincoln, near the Capitol. Often Bob would come up to our home on the reservation for the weekend since we'd need to be back in Lincoln Monday morning and have to parlay with Reuben and maybe the whole Tribal Council over the weekend.

I want to say here that the Winnebago Tribal Council was fantastic through this whole process. We could not have delivered the goods if the Tribal Council had not supplied the goods. If some senator or committee would throw us a zinger question on a Friday, we could count on the Tribal Council to have met and acted by Sunday night, so we could be in the Capitol responsively on Monday morning.

I don't know how many times that happened. But I do remember one late night Tribal Council meeting in the middle of the retrocession battle when, for other legal issues, Browning Pipestem flew in from D.C. with some bad news from Capitol Hill. At that particular time, the majority on the Tribal Council were women. One of them was Norma Stealer. When Browning laid out his tale of woe of yet another Washington action that hurt tribes, Norma, in late night exasperation, leaned across the Council table and said, "When does it end?" Browning, standing tall looked straight at her and said, "When you give up." I'll never forget the depth of the silence in that room in the moments that followed.

Bob and I decided we would meet with some key county officials to tell them what our client intended to do, and try getting some support. We started by making an appointment with the County Attorney, fella by the name of Stu Mills. For this meeting, we were joined by another

NARF attorney, Steve Moore, himself a veteran of some dicey but successful Indian rights issues in other states. We drove over to his office right on time at 11 one morning and laid out the whole story. We talked about the history of federal Indian policy, PL-280, retrocession and why the county should support it. We explained that it would save the state and county a lot of money if the Tribe had its own police force and court system. There would be an influx of federal money from the BIA which would circulate in the county. And there would be increased public safety because of tribal and BIA cops being based in the part of the county where most of the tribal folks lived instead of way over here at the county seat.

When we were done with our dog and pony show and had laid out all the logic and rationale, it was about noon. Bob asked Stu if he'd like to go across the street to the café for lunch with us. Stu said he didn't want to do that and, in fact, he wished that when we'd called to set up the appointment he would've told us to go fuck ourselves.

That turned out to be pretty much the county's official position. We called Sheriff Clyde Storie to set up a similar meeting to talk about the possibilities of cross-deputizing the Sheriff, his deputies and the Indian police so there'd be a seamless web of law enforcement to protect public safety. The Sheriff said there wasn't going to be any cross-deputization of officers because there wasn't going to be any retrocession, so there wasn't any need for a meeting.

The Thurston County Board of Supervisors did put us on their agenda and listened politely to our presentation. When we were done they thanked us for coming over and moved on to the next agenda item. When we got back to Walthill where my office was we pulled into a gas station. The proprietor came out to gas us up and said, "You the guys we're supposed to take our shotguns after?"

Although it really was that bad, there were some non-

Indians in Thurston County who listened, who understood and who even offered to help. And they did. When the legislature held field hearings on the reservation or committee hearings in the Capitol, there were always some supportive white county residents who testified they were not afraid of retrocession, were impressed with what the Tribe was doing generally and liked the idea of saving money and having increased law enforcement. They were clearly a minority of the non-Indian residents, but they were impressive and important to the Tribe's ultimate success.

Reuben Snake, besides being Tribal Chairman, was also at that time a major presence on the national Indian scene. He was the President of the National Congress of American Indians, he served on a variety of national committees and task forces, he was in demand as a speaker, and he was in further demand as a spiritual leader, being a highly respected Roadman in the Native American Church. Reuben had also about that time been nominated for a McArthur genius award and became a finalist for that prestigious prize.

None of this carried any weight with his detractors back home, of course, but it meant several things to Bob and me. It meant we had a dream client; a man of great wisdom and compassion with world class leadership abilities. It meant we had an articulate and authoritative spokesman whenever we needed one. It meant we had a client who gave us free reign to accomplish the task, and always gave us sage advice and guidance when we needed it. And he lived his life on the high moral ground, not a mean or vindictive bone in his body.

It also meant we couldn't have his daily time to pound the halls of the Unicameral, schmooze with the staffers and represent the Tribe in endless committee, agency and community meetings far from the reservation. So Reuben, using his shrewd political genius, gave us Louie LaRose to be our partner. Thus we had a core gang of three, committed to do whatever it took and sustained through the rough patches by a deep friendship and an ample amount of humor. I never knew stress could be so much fun.

As we lobbied the first year of this two-year battle, our opponents helped us. Bob, Louie and I would make our rounds, meeting with Senators and/or their staffers. At one level our message was a tough one to sell: we'd like the state to give up its jurisdictional authority over Indians on the Winnebago Indian Reservation. We had developed a well-oiled dog and pony show so we could emphasize appropriate key points depending on the audience. But still, that was a hard pill for the state to swallow. But then Clyde Storie got nervous and started making the same rounds of the Senators' offices. The next time we'd go back to those Senators' staffers they'd say, "Clyde was down here. Now we understand why the Winnebagos want retrocession." In other words, he was so bad he was good for us.

Louie didn't drink, but he could dance. Bob and I could do both, though neither perhaps very skillfully. Anyway, we became friends with some key staffers, lobbyists and press people in and around the Capitol. We had a full social life with them in the evenings and sometimes stayed till the band went home. We'd hear about Clyde, Stu Mills and other angry county folks coming down and inadvertently making our case to the more open-minded folks in Lincoln. We'd learn what issues were most important to what politicians, and with the help of the Winnebago Tribal Council, we'd be pro actively responsive to those issues.

It was a heady time. We gave it our all. NARF let Bob stay in Nebraska and supported him with whatever he needed. Louie never faltered. The Tribe couldn't afford to pay him (they weren't paying Bob or me either), but they did usually cover his expenses, although being on the outs politically within the Tribe, they sometimes made it hard for him. Fortunately, Reuben stood by him. Although they represented different political factions within the Tribe, Reuben knew how skilful and effective Louie could be, and I think he saw the persuasive chemistry and energy of our gang of three.

In spite of all that, we couldn't get it done in '85. Too many opponents, too many obstacles, too much fear of the Tribe. Too many lobbyists paid by the other side. In fact, at the end of the legislative session, we discovered that one of the two most influential lobbyists in the state had been quietly working against us gratis as a "favor" to Clyde. We were never sure why, though it may have something to do with Clyde having been President of the state Sheriff's Association. So we geared up more between legislative sessions. With Bob and NARF leading the way, we developed briefing papers, colored pie charts, the supportive interests of the Nebraska State Patrol, we educated the press some more, and we expanded the groundwork back in Winnebago.

One of our key arguments, particularly effective with the more conservative Senators, was the fiscal argument. It went generally like this: if the state gives up its jurisdiction, not only will that save the state a significant amount of money it spends for law enforcement, court expenses and incarcerations, but there will be a concomitant influx of federal funding to fill the void. But we had a problem constructing that argument because the federal Bureau of Indian Affairs (BIA) back in D.C. was bobbing and weaving and being noncommittal. We needed their written commitment desperately, not only so we could make a solid, credible fiscal argument on the economics of the matter, but also so there wouldn't be a scramble and a law enforcement void in the event we were successful. It was central to the integrity of the whole design that the BIA accept the retrocession offer and provide federal funding like they did with other tribes who were not under PL-280. Finally, in exasperation, Bob put on his tenacious bulldog hat and went to the top of the BIA and told them in no uncertain terms that unless they lived up to their treaty responsibilities and accepted their trust duty to accept the state's offer of retrocession and be present with law enforcement and court resources on the day retrocession became effective they were going to have blood on their hands. Bob is good. We got the federal commitment in writing.

In addition to all that, we did one other key thing. Bob persuaded NARF that the best hope we had of getting retrocession through the Unicameral in the second year was to hire a good lobbyist. Through NARF and the Tribe that's what we did. First off we offered that lobbyist who'd undermined our first year a small retainer primarily just to keep him from working against us. Then we hired the other most influential, respected, connected and well informed professional lobbyist in the Capitol and started anew. His name was Paul O'Hara. He had skill and integrity and was willing to make us a major priority client at a discounted price.

We also got some unexpected help. Stun guns were becoming popular with law enforcement, and Sheriff Clyde Storie had one. Clyde was beginning to feel boxed in and nervous about the Tribe winning this thing. He was getting some bad press, and his stonewalling strategy was raising questions back home when it was learned that the State Patrol was meeting with the Tribe and the BIA to talk about how they could cross-train and cross-deputize each others' officers if the Winnebagos were successful in persuading the state to retrocede, or return, the state's jurisdiction to the feds.

As I mentioned, Clyde Storie was sensitive about his height and liked to overcompensate with bluster and belligerence. Louie decided to cut him back down to size, if you will, by giving him the "Indian name" of Walking Small. We never called him that to his face; in fact, through all this we almost never spoke to him at all. But it was pretty certain that Clyde knew of his Indian name.

Totally unrelated to Winnebago retrocession (except in the sense that Clyde was starting to unravel), a dispute arose between Clyde and the Chief of Police in a town in the next county over. Clyde called this Chief of Police at home and they had a heated argument during which the Chief of Police called Clyde a "fucking shrimp." Clyde had no jurisdiction in that neighboring county, but he got in his Thurston County Sheriff's car and raced over to the Chief of Police's house in the next county and confronted him on his front porch. The Chief of Police told Clyde he was out of his jurisdiction and to get back in his car and go home. Clyde responded by pulling out his stun gun and dropping the Chief of Police.

Man, you can't get any better press than what came out of that incident. The political cartoonist for the Lincoln Journal had a field day: a great cartoon with the caption "Thurston County, Home of Stun Gun Justice. The whole shocking Storie... Clyde that is!"

The press interviewed Louie LaRose in print and on TV. Louie said he was shocked and indignant. He said it's just not right what Clyde did. That stun gun was supposed to be used on Indian people, and Clyde had no business going out of the county and using it on a white guy!

Then a white farm woman who lived in Thurston County, but not on the Winnebago Reservation, got into it. She actually lived and farmed on the Omaha Indian Reservation which had gone through retrocession 15 years earlier, back when it was relatively easy to do. This lady was the President of the Farm Bureau for that area of the state. She started going down to the Capitol making the rounds of the Senators' offices and insinuating that she was there in her official capacity on behalf of the Farm Bureau to urge them to vote against Winnebago retrocession – for all the typically misleading and fearful reasons every redneck in the area had trotted out, mostly variations on two themes: either "the Indians need us to govern them," or "the Indians will treat us unfairly if they have control."

When our friends in the Unicameral told us about this, Bob got his tenacious bull dog hat on (as opposed to his Eddie Haskell hat under which he was equally adroit and effective). Bob tracked down the head of the Farm Bureau who was vacationing in Florida at the time and told him of the lobbying going on in the name of the Farm Bureau. Bob asked if the Farm Bureau had a dog in this fight. Had they taken an official position? Had they authorized this lady to lobby in their name? Was he aware of the ethical rules associated with lobbying the state legislature? Getting the answers he hoped for, Bob demanded that this fellow call this woman up and instruct her to return to each and every office she had visited in the Capitol and retract or "clarify" her position by stating that, in fact, the Farm Bureau had not taken any position on this proposed legislation. You go, Bob!

Meanwhile, Bob, Louie and I had done our homework and refined our presentation. We could go in to talk to a Senator knowing what key points to emphasize to him or her and take turns speaking in such a way that I think we'd sometimes even finish each other's sentences. But once in a while we'd run into the unexpected and it'd make us wonder if there was any hope at all. For instance, one day we had an appointment with one of the senior statesmen of the Unicameral, a respected Senator with a thick head of white hair, fine suits and large office. The three of us thought we knew his interests and concerns and we went into that meeting prepared. We gave our whole pitch in about 20 minutes, emphasizing points we knew were of concern to him. He sat behind his large desk leaning back in his chair listening politely. Our timing was great. We knew he had another meeting, so we finished leaving just enough time for him to ask some questions. He only had one. He leaned forward over his desk and asked, "Tell me gentlemen, can Indians vote?"

The 1986 session of the Unicameral wore on. It was full-tilt-boogie and we were in warrior mode... but it was uncertain. One day we'd think we had the votes, and the next day we'd hear of some new fear mongering or a Senator's new concern and we'd be scrambling again. Anybody who's been through a contentious legislative process like this knows the emotional roller coaster that it is – including for the Winnebago people back on the reservation who had to listen to all this fearful and demeaning garbage being said about them. We were embarrassed for them.

Because the Nebraska legislature is a Unicameral, having only one body comprised of 49 Senators, you need 25 votes to win. After all the committee hearings, fact findings, expert testimony, battles in the press, including many editorials on both sides, after all the lobbying and brokering, a day was finally set for the Nebraska legislature to vote, up or down, on whether the state of Nebraska was going to ask the federal government to take back its jurisdictional authority on the Winnebago Indian Reservation, thus divesting the state of its authority and its responsibilities for criminal jurisdiction over Indians on that reservation.

Winnebago was abuzz. Buses were chartered and filled. Families piled into vans. Two nonstop years in the making, this was it. The Winnebagos arrived early and filled most of the seats in the upper balcony that wrapped around and looked down on the Senate floor. It was standing room only. The spillover crowd was milling around the Rotunda outside the Senate Chamber. Folks on all sides of the issue and lots of press. Anyone who read a newspaper knew this was the day. Camera crews were setting up in the corners for interviews, no matter what happened. It's worth saying that of all those Indian faces in the balcony, most belonged to older Winnebago women. Women who had experienced what Clyde Storie had done to their husbands, their children or nephews. Women who understood how critical it was to win this moment in order to reclaim control of their culture and their future. Neola Walker, the quintessential grand old lady of Winnebago, was in the building.

The floor debate was at times quite eloquent, and indeed it was long. Senators challenged each other's facts and even questioned each other's motives. Senators Ernie Chambers, Vard Johnson, Jim Pappas and others would not let the nay sayers win any cheap shots. Back and forth, exceeding the time limits set for debate. There were audible groans from the balcony when someone would challenge the Tribe's motives or capacities. Finally, the moment came, the debate was called to an end and each Senator – they were all there this day – had to push an electronic button, either a red one or a green one, and the tallies appeared on a big electronic board in the front of the Chamber. Many voted slowly and deliberately. Some seemed to wait to see what a trusted colleague was going to do. Others punched their answer in quickly. The building totals went back and forth. The Winnebagos were winning, then they were losing, then they were winning again. When it was over, it was over. The Winnebagos had won by a vote of 25 to 24.

When the Yeas hit 25, loud shrill ululations (warrior cries) erupted from the Winnebago women in the balcony. I'm sure there had never been such a sound filling that Chamber. Nearly every Senator looked up somewhat startled.

Recess was declared. The balcony emptied out, the Senate floor emptied out, the Rotunda filled. Neola Walker and all those other Winnebago women were crying and smiling and hugging their lawyers who were also crying and smiling as the gravity of the moment took hold.

The Winnebago people had, as a practical matter, just taken back a goodly amount of power to control their own lives on their own lands. Once the civil rights heyday had ended in the early 70's, I don't think any tribe in the country had done what Winnebago partnering with Nebraska's best had just accomplished.

The Rotunda was buzzing. The press was looking for spokespeople. In the middle of all this, I watched Louie LaRose walk up to Sheriff Clyde Storie and extend his hand. Clyde, I think just as a reflex, responded by extending his hand. Louie shook the Sheriff's hand and, as he did so, said, "Clyde, we couldn't have done it without you." Clyde withdrew his hand and walked away. He appeared to be stunned by the witty truth of what Louie just told him. Clyde had nothing. His reign of racist belligerence was over. His hard line defiance left him with no power over the Winnebagos, and no cooperative agreements to protect public safety such as had been worked out between the Tribe, the BIA and the State Patrol. And Clyde had let down his base of power – all the rednecks that supported him in election after election for 19 years were looking at Sheriff Walking Small differently. He was an embarrassment. Elections were coming up. There was blood in the water.

The way we had written the retrocession legislation, its effective date was set some months ahead. We did this to give everyone ample time after the vote to gear up for all the changes that would occur. There had to be cops, dispatchers, cars, equipment, radio frequencies and towers, the nuts and bolts of the state/tribal agreements. And there had to be tribal laws enacted and what had been just a children's court had to become a full fledged judicial system. There had to be a place to put prisoners and a tribal Court of Appeals.

The Winnebago Tribe, as we had assured the state they would, did all that and more. It was like a new era had dawned on the reservation. The old era of outside oppression and internal helplessness was over. The Winnebagos were in charge. The responsibilities were huge and well met. This was history in the making, which, as any Winnebago will tell you, calls for a little humor.

On July 1, 1986, when Winnebago retrocession went into effect, there was a ceremony. Bob Peregoy flew in from Colorado, and as he and Louie and I were standing around talking about how we'd just won the biggest battle of our lives and changed history, a news reporter came up to Louie with a cameraman and a mike and said, "Mr. LaRose, now that the state laws no longer apply here, what does this historic moment mean to you and your people?" Louie, without missing a beat, looked at him with a straight face and said, "It means we can finally tear those tags off the pillows and mattresses."

After all we'd been through that was such an outrageously clever nonsequitor that Bob and I had to hang on to each other to keep from falling down laughing.

POSTSCRIPT

There is one more thing that had to be done. Even though Clyde had lost his power over Indians, he was still the Sheriff of Thurston County and there were quite a few white folks there over whom he still had authority. Some of those folks met with tribal leaders from both tribes in Thurston County, the Winnebagos and the Omahas, and came up with a plan to find a good and decent candidate to run against Clyde in the upcoming election.

They found such a candidate in the person of Harold

Obermeyer. Harold had been Sheriff decades before and was remembered as a fair and reasonable man. He was now living in another county so a delegation of non-Indians went to meet with him, urge him to come back and run, and promise their support. Harold finally agreed, and folks got hopeful.

But it turned out there was one little problem. Clyde was a Republican and it was assumed he'd get the Republican nomination. Everyone thought Harold would run as the Democratic candidate, and that since most of the Indians were Democrats, he'd have a good chance of beating Clyde in a general election with the support of the anti-Clyde white folks.

Besides having a reputation for being fair, Harold Obermeyer also had a reputation for being stubborn. He said he'd been a Republican all his life and he wasn't about to change that now. A fellow with limited experience and somewhat of a criminal record signed up to run as a Democrat, but he had no chance. This meant that whoever won the Republican primary, Clyde or Harold, would be the next Sheriff of Thurston County.

There was only one way that Clyde Storie could be beaten in a Republican primary in Thurston County. That was if all the Indians would switch over and become Republicans and then show up and vote for Harold. Well, that's what they did. With the good cooperation of the Thurston County Clerk's Office, both tribes conducted a voter registration drive which included the element of becoming a Republican.

There were Indians lined up in front of both the Omaha and Winnebago tribal offices signing up as Republicans. Clyde heard about this and, in a last desperate and somewhat pathetic gasp, took out a full page ad in the local newspaper where in a kind of rant he said it was un-American to switch parties.

Clyde lost. Befitting his character, his departure was rather furtive and messy involving questions about county property – including the Sheriff's car. They eventually found the Sheriff's car in the parking ramp at the Omaha airport 80 miles away, but Clyde and his family were by that time in Florida and never came back.

An Abbreviant History of Western Civilization

A group by the small round sea
beat up a smaller group
which made the first group somehow bigger
And they went to the next peninsula
and hurt the peninsula people
until the peninsula people became like them
together, more or less,
somewhat mutted. In some rough
and tenuous quasi-synchronous disrootedness
When they came to the hinterlands
they ate and took over.
They conquered most of whom they encountered
converting until they were only fighting themselves
Pushing off to the next place
because they couldn't stand what they'd created
nor what they had destroyed
They killed and co-opted in every peopled place
and peopled with themselves each oasis
Over time
chasing themselves into a large corner
where the differences were all removed or eaten
and diseases increased
just like they would in a family or an acre
So this long since by now majoritarian group
that seems competent to neither
transform nor even decelerate bad habits
from time to time still concocts a reason

to squash a remaining culture
which has sustained an identity through traditional
time
and which thank god resists
sometimes with success.

Note to the reader: This account of PL-280, Indian law and Winnebago retrocession, should be read as a personal account in story style. It is not a full legal or factual accounting assessment – although that would make a great book and a full length motion picture. For a full treatment of PL-280 see Carole Goldberg-Ambrose's book "Planting Tail Feathers," published by UCLA in 1997.

Reburial in Nebraska

n the spring of 1987, Dennis Hastings came to my office in Walthill on the Omaha Indian Reservation. Dennis was sort of the unofficial Omaha tribal historian. He was a member of the Omaha Tribe, had a degree in anthropology and from time to time got some modest grants that allowed him to work in historic preservation.

Dennis was troubled. He'd been piecing together information that indicated there were a lot of dead Indian bodies being held in various Nebraska institutions, primarily the Nebraska State Historical Society (NSHS) and the University at its main campus in Lincoln.

The issue is basically this: Who speaks for the dead? Who has the right to decide how their graves, their bodies and their funerary objects are treated? The Native philosophies are generally quite simple: the dead are respectfully buried along with any appropriate funerary objects and left there to rest in peace for eternity. Pretty straight forward, similar to most contemporary beliefs and practices.

Unfortunately, history is a lot messier. For a variety of reasons, most of them unsavory, Indian graves have been dug up and looted from the 19th Century right up to this very day, although it is fortunately much less common now.

Many Indian graves were dug up in the 19th Century under a policy of the military. They wanted Indian crania to study in some strange effort to measure intelligence, and they paid for the heads. In other cases, it has been science that has been generally interested in studying all aspects of "pre-historic" life and routinely played "finders keepers" with any skeletal remains they came across through road building, erosion or intentional "digs." In many other cases, right up to the present, it is simply a matter of grave robbers. These are folks who dig up dead Indians and traffic in the bones and the burial goods. Often these bodies and goods have wound up in respectable institutions – such as the Nebraska State Historical Society.

I told Dennis I'd help him. It seemed to me there were some legal issues here, in addition to the moral ones. We learned fairly readily that the State Historical Society had hundreds of bodies, which they didn't want to talk with us about, and that the circumstances through which they got these bodies were murky. We also learned that several other states were beginning to address this issue, always at the instigation of affected tribes.

Nebraska has a state agency called the Nebraska Indian Commission. When we began, it was directed by Wallace Coffey (Comanche) and at the time we were done it was directed by Reba White Shirt (Mandan). Under their good leadership, the Commission was very helpful and supportive, and gave us access to its resources, including research request authority and office space in the Capitol building.

As we began to understand the history and scope of the problem we took a look at how these issues were being addressed in other states, such as the neighboring state of Kansas where just outside of Salina, for a fee, you could view dozens of Indian bodies in situ at the Indian Burial Pit, half exposed, but still in their graves. A roof had been put over the "dig."

We consulted, met with Indian elders for guidance and with the help of the Indian Commission, came up with a draft of legislation that would help tribes identify what remains were held by various state entities, their tribal affiliation and a method for returning those remains to their respective tribes upon request for reburial. We thought (naively) that if we had something to show the Historical Society, a skeletal (if you will) plan, it would give us something to work with and toward – a starting point.

The Executive Director of the NSHS at the time was a fellow by the name of Dr. James Hanson. Jim, as he liked to be informally called, was a big, robust, bearded man born and raised in Nebraska. He'd gone away to school and came home with a PhD and landed his ideal plum job running the NSHS. He was at the top of his game. Turns out he thought he was God's gift to pretty much everything, and when we showed him our working draft, he went ballistic with all the blustery arrogance he could muster. Instead of rolling up his sleeves to negotiate what might and might not work, he dug in his heels and immediately launched a campaign to discredit us.

It was shocking how opposition galvanized against us in spite of the fact that what we were trying to do was essentially rectify the desecration of graves. But Hanson, with help from the NSHS Board, rallied opponents with sensationalism, misinformation and deceit in a media campaign. It helped them that one of their Executive Board members was the publisher of the Omaha World Herald, the only paper of statewide distribution in Nebraska.

It became immediately clear that this was going to be another major Indian rights battle in Nebraska, and it was going to get ugly. I was still alone at the "Indian Desk" of the Legal Aid Office on the rez, and neither Dennis nor his tribe had enough resources to make this happen, particularly since it wasn't clear at that time how many Omaha Indians the state was hoarding above ground. I might've been foolish to jump into this alone, but I'd be foolish no longer. It was time to call in the big dogs. I called NARF and got Bob Peregoy and Walter Echo-Hawk interested. Later Steve Moore from NARF came into the fray, too. NARF quickly became the key force to end the desecration. Then for balance, grounding and humor, we went to the Winnebago Tribe and asked if they'd give us Louie LaRose. He, of course, loves a good fight and was interested in all of us working together again. The Winnebago Tribe, though not native to Nebraska, and, therefore, perhaps without any members' bodies in the "collections" nonetheless saw this as a fundamental Indian rights issue and, as I recall, committed at least some expense money to Louie. Turns out he would need it all and more, but the main thing at that point was: the team was back together and hot on the trail of what was right.

It was remarkable how hard this fight was, and that it took most of three years of persistent and thorough effort to get it done. The battle was in meetings between the Indians and the anthros, in legislative committee hearings, and increasingly in the press. In one angry exchange, Jim Hanson proclaimed in a loud voice, "Nothing is leaving the NSHS under my watch," to which I replied, "Oh yeah, where you gonna go then?"

We asked Jim Hanson how he'd like it if we dug up his grandmother, took her wedding ring, bible, whatever she might've been buried with, and put her bones on a shelf and her burial goods on display. He said that wouldn't bother him a bit as long as it was for science.

Well, this got Louie thinking, and he came up with an idea for the Winnebago White Museum. He said it would be part of a long ongoing attempt of the Indian people to study and understand the strange culture of white guys. He said in the displays, behind the glass, instead of pottery shards, there would be Tupperware. Louie always brought perspective, and the humor was priceless.

We couldn't believe the intransigence of the other side on an issue that, once exposed to the light of day, seemed so obvious in its result. We seriously considered a little theater. We talked about going down to Omaha or Lincoln and digging up some graves, using Louie's theory about employing this scientific methodology in order to better understand white people. In the end, we decided against this plan for one single reason: respect for the dead.

Meanwhile Hanson claimed NSHS had "title" to the dead bodies and had "bills of sale" from purchasing them. The general public was turning in our favor as a result, with some folks starting to refer to the "Nebraska State Hysterical Society."

One meeting between our side and the team of anthros and curators from NSHS was particularly poignant. We had studied the Rules of Ethics of the American Anthropology Association. Their ethical code says that whenever your anthro work interferes with an ongoing culture, you should defer to the culture you're studying and back off. And we had also learned by that point that the vast majority of Indian bodies held by the NSHS, some 360 or more, were Pawnee. We had also shared with NSHS statements from the Pawnee elders describing their belief that disinterred spirits were at unrest and this unresolved state of affairs was adversely affecting their current tribal culture.

At this meeting, it is important to note there were on our side of the table two Pawnees: Walter and Roger Echo-Hawk; Walter, an attorney for NARF, and Roger, a Tribal Historian and scholar.

So we reminded the anthros about the AAA's ethical rules and asked how they justified their actions of keeping these hundreds of bodies and burial goods in the face of those rules and what the Pawnees were telling them. They said it was simple: "the Pawnees we study are extinct." There was no conflict at all. Walter and Roger showed great composure and said nothing. In their silence, the historical trauma was palpable. Eventually, Peregoy and I couldn't take their glib explanation anymore and started ranting about their convenient and rationalized hypocrisy. It was to no avail.

Hanson brought in the national heavy hitter anthros who had been fighting repatriation (return for reburial) all over the country. We'd ask these guys what they'd learned from studying those disinterred dead Indians for over a hundred years. They'd say, well not much yet, but someday there may be a scientific breakthrough that will allow us to learn a lot – but only if we keep control of these bodies. Sometimes they'd answer vaguely that they'd learned what Indians ate before the white man showed up. Louie said, "You could'a just asked us."

We had a new bill in the legislative hopper the second year. We had conceded a few points to Hanson and his crowd in the drafting, but it was mainly our bill, and we had not sacrificed principle or respect for the dead. The battle heated up in the press and Jim Hanson came out calling us "book burners" for wanting to rebury the dead. I was on the Board of Directors of the Nebraska Civil Liberties Union at the time and on the Indian Rights Advisory Committee for the ACLU nationally. So I was pretty stunned at being called a book burner.

Legacy Dream

The heart is a kindly organ
The brain can go either way.

I wish I could say
My generation will leave the world
Better, safer
More harmonious
Than we found it.

Now, over half a century in

Such deep sadness
To find that not likely.

The soul is a gracious capacity
The brain can go either way.

The Pawnees filed an Open Records request in an attempt to ascertain what NSHS was hoarding so vigorously.
Hanson refused to comply. We went to the Nebraska Attorney General who issued an Opinion instructing him to
comply. Still Hanson refused and only acquiesced after a
second A.G. Order. The public was getting fed up with his
shenanigans and the op-ed pieces began to turn more our
way.

But Hanson and some of his Board and staff just got
more desperate. They went public claiming the Pawnees
were planning to sell the burial goods on the antiquities
market, or they were going to put all these reburial items
in their own museum. It was disgusting, but it was working in our favor. They formed a group called "Citizens to
Save Nebraska's History," but it was too late. Even though
the Pawnees were from Oklahoma and couldn't vote in Nebraska, the state legislators' own constituents were telling
them to do the right thing. Give them back their dead.

Hanson was starting to look stooped. He was a big
man, but something wasn't right with him. He started aging fast. Several old Indians had mentioned along the way
that Mr. Hanson shouldn't be doing what he was doing. It
was dangerous to his physical, mental and spiritual health.
He was messing with things he didn't understand, and
didn't respect in the proper way.

In the end we won. We got the Unmarked Human Burial Sites and Skeletal Remains Protection Act passed into
law on May 19, 1989. The first general repatriation law
in the country. We'd made our case well to the Nebraska
people, and they got it. They had written letters to the edi-

tors, they'd called their legislators; some of them had even actively lobbied for us. It felt good.

You might think I'm making this up, but even after we'd won, it wasn't over. Hanson, unbeknownst to his Board, filed a lawsuit claiming NSHS didn't have to comply with the new law because it only applied to public institutions and NSHS was not a state agency, but rather just a simple nonprofit corporation. At the trial it was shown they'd been a state agency by statute for 108 years, they got 75% of their funding from the state because they were a state agency, and they'd held themselves out all over the place as a state agency for fundraising and other purposes throughout their history. It was pathetic. Ironically, had they won that case they would've lost most of their funding and, in fact, owed the state a lot of money according to the state auditor. Fortunately for everyone they lost. Then they tried to promote a new bill that would amend the new law and allow them to keep all the burial goods. But the public and the Senators were exhausted with this issue by that time and the bill died in committee.

But that was just the beginning really. The real work was getting those Native bodies and their burial goods identified as to tribe, returned and reburied. The Pawnees, with the largest number of their ancestors disinterred and housed in Nebraska, went first. After nearly three bitterly fought years the day came (Sept. 7, 1990) when the Pawnees were to come to the NSHS and retrieve 401 bodies, each in its own little wooden coffin, built long enough for a femur (longest bone in the body), with the head at an identified end, burial goods included with the bones, and identifying information printed on the coffins. Identified chiefs and representatives of the various Pawnee clans were set aside and were put in a hearse first, filling it. Then we backed up to the NSHS loading dock the biggest Ryder rental truck we could find, and something like a procession began.

The NSHS staff brought the coffins to the loading dock and handed them over, one at a time, to those of us (Pawnees and friends) loading the truck. We stacked them carefully and we filled the truck almost exactly. It took much of the day. Jim Hanson, as I recall, was present when we showed up in the morning, but quickly disappeared. He did not help us with these human bodies that he coveted so much.

In the late afternoon when we just barely were able to close the truck door after loading the last of the coffins, something remarkable happened and, to this day, I don't know who caused it to happen. Two Lincoln Police cars pulled up and we formed a funeral procession -- a police car in the front with all its lights on, followed by the hearse with the chiefs' and clan leaders' coffins, then the big yellow Ryder truck, then numerous cars with Pawnees, other Indians and friends, then in the rear, the other Lincoln Police car, all lights on. We drove slowly through downtown Lincoln and as we passed each intersection downtown, there were police cars blocking off the side streets to give us the right-of-way. Moreover, at each of those intersections, the policemen were out of their cars standing at attention as we passed. Some with their hands to their foreheads in silent salute, others with their hands over their hearts; I wept as we slowly drove by.

The funeral procession proceeded to the highway at the edge of town. There, sitting at the city limits, were two Nebraska State Patrol cars waiting with all their lights on. The city police fell out and the State Patrol fell in, front and rear, and led us over a hundred miles out into rural Nebraska to the little town of Genoa where we arrived in the evening.

We pulled into a little motel where I think we had rented every room. We thanked the State Troopers and they went home. We posted a guard to watch over the dead and the rest of us slept till dawn.

We were in Genoa because of the kind heartedness of its citizens. Genoa, a little town out on the prairie, used to be Pawnee territory. In fact, there is an old Indian Boarding School there that, although now a locally run museum, is still the subject of stories in many Pawnee and other Indian families. The good folks of Genoa knew the horrors and indignities that had happened there and, over the years, had made welcome overtures to the Pawnee (now in Oklahoma) including trying their best to tell the truth at the Boarding School Museum.

Genoa had a cemetery outside of town. For this purpose they had donated enough room in their cemetery for a mass grave to hold all the Pawnee coffins... and they had dug the hole perfectly with a flat bottom and nice square corners. And the Genoans were there for us. The town leaders and others showed respect and support by offering speeches at the graveside and helping us lay those 401 Pawnees to rest.

But the folks in charge of this were the Pawnees, up from Oklahoma in large numbers – tribal leaders, elders, spiritual leaders, children and singers. And although the Pawnee made this strange event look almost normal, it wasn't. I know their leaders and everyone really struggled with this, and understandably so, for in the Pawnee culture there are no ceremonies for reburial because no one would ever dig up someone else's grave!

There were prayers, historical remembrance, the giving of thanks, many songs, cedar, sage and sweet grass smells filled the air. The drum beat, high pitched songs filled the cemetery and floated off over the prairie. When all the coffins were carefully placed stacked up in the mass grave with the head end of each casket facing East, Pawnee women brought out special Star Quilts they had made for this occasion. There must've been 20 of them. They spread them out so that quilts covered the grave, every coffin was under a quilt. They scattered other things on top – might've been cedar and sage. Then, with more songs the backhoe began to carefully scatter dirt over the grave until everything was covered over.

And over that mass grave the good people of Genoa helped frame and pour yet another layer – a thick concrete layer over the whole burial site. Within that cap of concrete they left long round holes that went down to the dirt below. The Pawnees wanted the rainy hand of Mother Nature to reach down and continue to touch and nourish and transform their relatives slowly through the long course of time. But those holes were not too big around, because the Pawnees did not want the hand of man to reach down again into the sanctity of their relatives' final resting place. Now it was done.

Jim Hanson had to leave the NSHS and, in fact, left town. He never knew we had a mole at NSHS; a man on his staff with a heart and perspective. When we began clandestinely meeting with him we dubbed him "Paleo Man," because he was the first true human being we had found at NSHS. He gave us valuable inside information throughout, and his kind soul encouraged us through this sad but noble task.

The Board at NSHS went through some changes too. Some, such as Roger Welsch, had jumped ship early on as this story developed. Roger was a well-known and well-read personality in Nebraska. It was significant as a barometer of public morality that Roger felt compelled to not only disassociate himself from NSHS, but also actively assist us in our efforts. Years later Roger gifted much of his Nebraska farm to the Pawnee Tribe of Oklahoma. Others on the NSHS Board had lost either credibility or heart as it went on. Things changed. In November of '91 the new leadership of NSHS announced their intention to fully comply with the spirit of the law saying, "We are out of the bones business."

That Nebraska law, partly because of all the care and attention we were forced to apply to it, was well-written, comprehensive and many said the best of its kind in the country. Walter Echo-Hawk and others were just getting national momentum for a similar federal law. So Walter took our Nebraska law with him to D.C. and it served as the model for the Native American Graves Protection and Repatriation Act (NAGPRA) which was passed by Congress in 1991.

This generally successful story must regrettably not end without it being said that NAGPRA still meets with resistance in its implementation. What century is this where we still can't honor the dead with the basic modicum of respect implicit in the phrase "rest in peace?"

Pallbearers for the Pawnee

Beneath the lightning and the halfmoon
of September 1990
We gathered in a hotel room in Lincoln
preparing to do what was undone.

Overcoming the hostile forces
of misguided power, racial conceit
and some tragic history
Nebraska last year made landmark law
for the repatriation of human remains
and burial goods, looted from the Earth
throughout many decades of the Nineteenth
and Twentieth Centuries.

After a late night prayer
and nearly four years of steady effort

we had come to retrieve the new wood coffins
of four hundred and one Pawnee
Beginning in the early morning
with coffins piled high up long hall walls
we carried them out of the institution
out of view of the press conference
all day long and into the waning light.
Pallbearers to the Pawnee
Louie, Steve, Paleo and I
carried those coffins in our arms
and stacked them up to the roof
of a big yellow truck
and filled the long white hearse.

25NC3
S 37
the coffin says
and on the inventory list
 female, young adult
Circling the cars around in the sunset
and falling into line
the procession leaves the museum
and heads west slow through town
police escort front and rear
followed by the hearse
the long slow truck
and half a dozen cars.
At the major intersections
police cars lights flashing red and blue
blocked off traffic,
the officers stood at still attention
their right hands over their hearts
Passing through those intersections
I broke down and wept, for humanity
for the deep and humble sorrow of knowing,
for a vague faith in humanity

for the clear poetic beauty
of this particular sunset
I wept for human confusion
and for the joy of peace.

In those moments contempt fell dead
but its strength remains in resolve.

From the edge of the city
the State Patrol leads us west
into a lightning lit horizon
the funeral procession one hundred miles long
rolls slowly into the night
decades after the fact.
Wending our way through the two-lane plains
Arriving late to meet a patient town board
and to rest.

The good people of Genoa Nebraska
welcomed us with open arms
in the spirit of the Golden Rule
with a kind and religious respect.
If we are the human family
then everyone who's gone before
is my ancestor, somebody said.

Next morning gathering up around the mass grave
pallbearers in the grass of the morning sun
handing coffin after coffin
to pallbearers in the hole
placing them gently east to west.
A star quilt
shawls and blankets
looking beautiful and warm
are spread out over the coffins,
and the sands of time lay down to rest again

with an offered prayer
for the spirits of their people
and for us all
from the Pawnee people
who with informed and straight ahead dignity
conducted the entire proceeding without
precedent.

And finally we stood
around hot coals in an empty room
at the old Genoa Indian School
where a eagle feather fanned
the living cedar smoke
with a prayer
and it was done.

For a full treatment of this issue of the repatriation of Indian remains from a national perspective, see "Battlefields and Burial Grounds" by Roger Echo-Hawk and Walter Echo-Hawk, Lerner Publishing, 1994. For a full blow-by-blow accounting of this battle in Nebraska see "The Legal Basis, Legislative History, and Implementation of Nebraska's Landmark Reburial Legislation," by Robert Peregoy, Arizona State Law Journal, Vol. 24, No. 1, Spring 1992.

Making "The Peyote Road"
a tribute to Rhino

My dear friends Gary Rhine and Phil Cousineau always loved a good story. Here's one about how they helped shape history.

On April 19, 1990, the U.S. Supreme Court in a case called Employment Division of Oregon v. Smith ruled that the First Amendment's guarantee of Free Exercise of Religion would no longer be interpreted as broadly as in the past and, in particular, an old Indian religion that had its 10,000 year old roots in the Americas, and now with a quarter of a million Native American adherents would not be protected. For this religion called the Native American Church to be protected by the Constitution was, in the words of Justice Scalia, "a luxury our democracy can no longer afford."

Those frightfully chilling words stunned the 250,000 Native Americans who, in practicing the religion of their forefathers and mothers, had essentially been made into felons overnight.

The next morning, on April 20, 1990, one of the great Native American leaders of the 20th Century, Reuben Snake, Jr. of the Winnebago Tribe of Nebraska, began the effort to make things right. Native American Church members of the neighboring Omaha Tribe met that day and, recognizing his wisdom and abilities, called him over to a meeting and asked him to do something to save this venerable old religious tradition that was central to all their lives. Then Reuben came to my office, looked me in the eye and said,

"Brother, help me with this."

I knew the case and the result. I reminded him that I ran a little one attorney Indian legal aid program with a $28,000 a year budget, $15,000 of which was my salary. I also mentioned that I knew he was broke, in fact his home phone had been recently disconnected. Although he was highly respected as a national Indian leader and the Chairman of the Winnebago Tribe of Nebraska, the Tribe too was barely getting by financially. Trying not to overstate the dilemma, I reminded him that we were two poor individuals living on an Indian reservation and rather unlikely to succeed in overturning a decision of the U.S. Supreme Court. Reuben said we simply had to try, there was no viable alternative and, with a twinkle in his eye, he looked at me reassuringly and said, "We'll find good friends along the way."

We went to see Senator Daniel Inouye who was at that time Chair of the Senate Committee on Indian Affairs. Sen. Inouye, a bright man with real heart, listened and empathized. We told him we wanted his help in passing a law that would specifically protect the rights of Indian people to use Peyote sacramentally in the practice of this venerable old religion. Senator Inouye knew the story of what the Supreme Court had done, and was well aware of the Native American Church. He said we were unlikely to succeed. Reuben said we must succeed. The Senator said the only chance we had would require a massive public education process about Peyote and the NAC.

After the meeting Reuben said he'd recently learned of a filmmaker, Gary Rhine, and his writer friend, Phil Cousineau, who had made a very sensitive, accurate and well-received documentary called Wiping the Tears of Seven Generations. He thought they might be the ones for this project. The whole venture seemed so far fetched that I just mumbled something about a need to meet these two and how it would probably be more work to educate the filmmakers than it was worth.

Reuben set up a meeting with them at the Albuquerque Airport. I'll never forget that day. Reuben and I flew in first and were standing around in Baggage Claim waiting for these two unknowns to arrive. Finally, a new plane load of passengers started coming down the escalator and in that crowd two guys stood out. I watched them coming and looked at Reuben and said, "If that's them, this is going to work."

Needless to say, that was them. And there was no learning curve, they were warrior ready. From that meeting came the award winning documentary "The Peyote Road", and thereafter victory in Congress for the NAC. It wasn't that simple, of course. It was a four year obsession that kept many of us on the road far too much. It was a real life saga that left a mark on all of us who lived and breathed this enormous effort. Against all odds we were able to essentially overturn a decision of the U.S. Supreme Court by persuading a majority of Congress to enact a law that protects the right of Indian people to use, possess and transport Peyote for their religious purposes anywhere in the U.S.A. no matter what other federal or state laws may say about controlled substances.

Two of the heroes of this moral and legal victory were Gary Rhine and Phil Cousineau, about whom not enough has been said. Senator Inouye was right, in order to have any chance at all with such a controversial issue we, at the very least, would have to educate legislators and their staff, policy makers, scholars, clergy, educators and philanthropists. Even, to a certain extent, Indian Country. This educational process was also important to steal the thunder of any potential detractors who might want to sabotage our efforts with misinformation.

Gary and Phil got all this. They were a godsend . . .

a seasoned godsend. They went about making the film in just the right way, sensitive to every issue, humble as need be and careful to check-in with the real mastermind of the whole effort, Reuben Snake, at every juncture. Everywhere we went, there was Gary with his camera. And that was just for starters. He made dozens of special trips to sometimes hard to get to places all over the country to get interviews and other footage that someone said was important. Tireless, selfless, committed and, equally important, fairly well-funded. Some few folks out there believed in this effort and had well-placed trust in Gary and Phil. This was hugely important because we were moving around a lot in those days to cover all the bases and we were doing it on what Reuben called "a frequent flyer coupon and a prayer."

So the film came together at a specific length of something like 57 minutes which is what one would want if one hoped to get it on PBS or other hour-based television. It got printed and sent to everywhere we could think it needed to go for our purposes. Sometimes Gary or Phil or another of us would go with it to speak before and after the showing. Although it eventually won awards and was shown on many PBS stations, before we got it distributed at all, we learned we had a problem.

We showed it to some of our friends in D.C. They were hugely impressed with both the quality and the content. But they said, for a lobbying tool in D.C. it wouldn't work - too long. No one in D.C. has an attention span beyond 10, 12 or, at the outside, 15 minutes. If you can't say it in that amount of time, no one wants to hear it.

There was only one logical thing to do, take The Peyote Road back into the editing room, chop it down to its essential essence and produce a version we secretly called "The Peyote Shortcut." That version served its purpose well with the folks in D.C., and together those two versions played a significant role in our victory, while also creating a record for posterity.

"The Peyote Road" is an important film. It's one of those rare films that you can say with confidence actually helped change the world, make it a better place. And it only worked because Gary and Phil were so good at what they do. The whole project was driven by respect and told in a way that the people living on the Peyote Road participated in and approved of. This was filmmaking and writing at its best.

So with the help of the film, the friends, the Peyote and the prayers, on October 6, 1994, a corrective act was signed into law by the President of the United States and a beautiful and vital spiritual way of life had its legal dignity restored.

And while the rest of us were celebrating that event, Gary and Phil had the joyful task of going back into the editing room one more time to update the story ... to make it a movie with a happy ending.

More films and books followed for Gary and Phil, each with its own noble purpose; each made with selfless love, good humor and a keen sense of justice by two remarkable men.

Gary, in one of those awful tragic moments that just pulls the rug out from under your feet, died in a plane crash in 2006 while teaching someone how to fly. As for Phil, hell, he is so busy writing, publishing, speaking, guiding and coaching little league baseball for his son's team, you can barely get him on the phone... but he's right there with you when you do.

This whole story about what the Supreme Court did to this beautiful, humble old religion, and about the triumph in the end got quite a lot of attention, and many of us who worked on it were honored in one way or another. I just wanted to give a little extra recognition to Gary and Phil.

Reuben Saw

Once in a near ago time
A large aging man prayed
put his mind on the Creator
"talked to God."
This big brown eyed man could see
how good things and bad things
came to pass
and where they might lead.
Through that he was full of love
with which he honored Creation
in its seamless dancing relentlessness.
Through that he was full of respect
knowing all things are related
and come from God.
Through that he was full of compassion
because he could see
the forgetfulness and the pain
people make.
Such a strong man
extended his love
expressed his vision
and passed to the spirit world.

Not many people know.

The story of the Smith case and the amazing legislative victory four years later essentially overturning that god awful decision is well told by another hero of that battle, Walter Echo-Hawk of NARF in his new book "In the Courts of the Conquerors: The Ten Worst Indian Law Cases Ever Decided", Fulcrum Press, 2010. A further accounting of this multiyear saga is described in "One Nation Under God" by Huston Smith and Reuben Snake, published by Clear Light Publishers in 1996.

A Tribute To Reuben Snake

MY MENTOR

When I got out of law school and got my first lawyering job at age 35 I had this green feeling like I hadn't had since I first sat in Buddhist meditation half my life ago. Armed with three college degrees I went to meet my first client, a "reservation Indian" with no college degrees. His name was Reuben Alvis Snake, Jr., and he was Chairman of the Tribal Council of the Winnebago Tribe of Nebraska. He was wearing blue jeans and so was I. He said he'd been waiting for me. Since I'd never heard of him before that week I wasn't sure what he meant. He took me under his wing (no small thing for a snake!) and before long he was introducing me to senators, governors, and medicine men. He wanted some legislation passed in Nebraska to protect the rights of Indians. With his guidance it got done. He wanted the Congress to essentially overturn a bad decision of the U.S. Supreme Court in order to protect and respect his beloved Native American Church. With his guidance it got done. Reuben put victories in my resumé and gray hairs in my mustache. He started as my client, became my friend, adopted me as his brother, and became Uncle Reuben to my kids. Through it all he was my mentor. He taught me, no, he showed me respect for absolutely everything, the value of relationships, the power of love in the rough-and-tumble world and how with humility, grace and a healthy dose of humor, one can change the course of history. Reuben died in 1993, and since then I've only seen him in my dreams. He came a couple of times shortly after passing into the spirit world, bringing compassion and some last advice.

I was lucky. I was blessed. My mentor was my best friend. Not everyone has it that way. I'm over 60 now. People think I know what I'm doing. But when I have a tough challenge or decision in front of me, in the quiet of my mind I'm thinking, "What would Reuben do?" Then I'm guided by his presence – or maybe it's my own inner sense associated with him. I can't tell the difference anymore. That means the mentoring worked.

A version of the tribute above was first published in "Once and Future Myths, the Power of Ancient Stories in Modern Times," by Phil Cousineau, Conari Press, 2001. Reprinted with permission of the author. For a more fulsome look at this remarkable man see his autobiography "Reuben Snake, Your Humble Serpent" as told to Jay C. Fikes, Clear Light Publishers, 1996. I had the good fortune of being asked to write the Foreword to that book, which is reprinted with permission in edited fashion below.

"If we don't change our direction,
We're going to wind up where we're heading."

With those words of what he liked to call "Winnebago Wisdom," Reuben Snake gently nudged the hearts and minds and spirits of all who had ears to hear him... and there were many.

Some few people seem to have the ability to see the whole world at once, to see across all the chasms and through all the obstacles that occupy so much of our daily lives. Few indeed have the ability to see through time, to live knowingly as the embodiment of all that has gone before and simultaneously as the compassionate giant who selflessly prepares a high road for the journeys of future generations.

You are about to read the story of such a man. It is a humble story because he tells it himself. In this book, you will not find a litany of his accomplishments because that was neither his purpose nor his style. Besides, if someone were to begin today to recite the many good things Reuben Snake did in this world, the time it would take could be counted in seasons.

Jay Fikes has very thoughtfully used the trust Reuben placed in him to illuminate the astonishing transformations Reuben made in his lifetime. Reuben's spiritual journey exemplifies hope, demonstrating how he overcame the prejudice and abuse which were directed toward most Indians of his generation. But this book provides more than mere testimonial about individual redemption. Reuben Snake emerged from an archetypal passage. Having learned the lessons taught by suffering and injustice, he rose up to become a champion of his people.

Reuben said that his grandfather told him there are three things that make the enjoyment of human life possible – three things that people should try to exhibit in their everyday lives. Respect. Compassion. Honor.

Here is what Reuben Snake said about them a few years back.

> *Respect:* "Each one of us is endowed by the Creator with his spirit. The spirit that makes you stand up and walk and talk and see and hear and think is the same spirit that exists in me – there's no difference. So when you look at me, you're looking at yourself – and I'm seeing me in you."

Compassion: "When you look at all the other parts of creation, all the other living creatures – the Creator endowed them with gifts that are far better than ours. Compared to the strength of the grizzly bear, the sharp sightedness of the eagle, the fleetness of the deer, and the acute hearing of the otter, we're pitiful human beings. We don't have any of those physical attributes that the Creator put into everything else. For that reason, we have to be compassionate with one another and help one another – to hold each other up."

Honor: "It's easy to point fingers at one another for our shortcomings, but to show somebody the feelings of pride that you have in them for what they do that's beneficial to their fellow man – that takes effort. But if you go to that kind of effort, then you're going to have that good feeling that we have to have one for another. And that's what makes life enjoyable."

These are the kinds of teachings, the depth of understanding that wise men and women have spoken of for thousands of years from all the great spiritual traditions of the world. Reuben was right up there with all those great sages, patiently waiting for the rest of us. Each and every being is brought into Creation by the great mysterious power we in some languages call God; each being embodies the sacred gift of life, yet each and every one is unique. So many times I saw how Reuben respected all the beings in Creation, how he honored them, how he showed compassion with his skilful and humorous patience for the problems of daily life that so many brought to his door.

He was such a huge man. His mind was in the spirit world of the Creator, his feet compassionately on Mother Earth, his heart flowing freely in between. Some few people throughout time have had the ability to talk of the important things of life from a place of understanding. Reuben was one of the precious few of those who not only spoke that way, but lived it.

Through his story, Reuben gently nudges us to realize that if we are true to our spiritual bearings, if we live our lives with respect, compassion, and honor, and if we are thereby guided to do things in this world, we can and do change the course of the future we leave for our children. You've heard about the stereotype... herein you can listen to the archetype.

Lest the reader feel that I am exaggerating the man, consider this: How many of us are able to accomplish transforming our vision of the world we want to live in into the policy and law of the United States? In his Afterword to this book, Walter Echo-Hawk succinctly describes the history of legal and political oppression perpetrated against Indian people – particularly in the area of religious expression, and most pointedly against Reuben's beloved Native American Church.

The horrendous injustice committed by the U.S. Supreme Court in permitting the practice of this venerable spiritual tradition to be criminalized in American law stirred Reuben to his last courageous fight. I will never forget the day after that dreaded decision in the *Smith* case in April of 1990 when Reuben asked me to help him "overturn the ruling of the Supreme Court."

When I reminded him that neither he nor the Native American Church had any of the money or resources necessary for such a daunting task, he smiled broadly and said, "We'll find good friends along the way." When I reminded him of his poor health, his expression grew stern and he said it was something that simply must be done. He looked at me and said, "I'll give the rest of my life to this if I have to."

Reuben was right. There were good, strong, committed friends along the way... enough to accomplish the task. And he was also right on the other count. He quit his job and committed himself to his final battle. With prayers by night and work by day he poured his energy into this seemingly impossible task. In the end, he gave it more energy than he actually had and died along the way, but not before he had singularly and clearly set the wheels in motion that resulted in a strong new federal law that ended literally hundreds of years of persecution against the peyote religion. His essential and catalytic efforts helped restore this ancient way of worship to the dignified place it deserves among the profound spiritual traditions of the world.

Even though he was a prayerful man, Reuben believed in rolling up your sleeves and getting things done in a responsible way. He often illustrated the point by telling the story of the family whose home was about to be flooded by a swollen river. First a truck came down the road urging the people to get in and be taken to higher ground. The family declined, saying they believed in God and that he would take care of them and see to their needs. The water rose up to the ground floor of their home and a boat came by calling for the family to get in and ride to safety. Again, they declined and climbed to their roof. A helicopter came overhead to lower a rope to them, but the family said again that they were putting their faith in God who would take care of them. Finally the waters rose over the roof and the family was swept away. When they got to Heaven, they cried out, "Dear God, we put all our faith in you and yet were swept to our deaths! How could you do this to us?"

To which God replied, "Hey! I sent you a truck and a boat and a helicopter. You have to do something too!" Reuben Snake did something too.

What an honor it was not only to know Reuben, but to go out and fight the good fight with him for the last ten years of his life as his lawyer, his friend, and his adopted brother. Because of his vision and his wisdom, he chose the fights worth fighting, and because of the respect he engendered he found friends in both likely and unlikely places, and he prevailed. His people prevailed. Righteousness prevailed.

Whether it was in accomplishing the thousands of little things few will ever remember, or whether it was undertaking the huge battles that I sometimes thought were too big, it was an unspeakable honor to have walked beside him – one step behind. Reuben showed us all how to overcome evil and ignorance with dignity and compassion. Such are the ways of a Warrior Sage.

Reuben Snake had the good fortune to be born into a culture that is rooted in the perennial values, the old ways. He had the intellectual capacity and the presence of being to understand the spiritual truths within those ways. I watched those understandings wash right through him, as if he were passing them from the past to the future – and indeed, he was. This Sweet Earth has never had a better friend.

When Reuben passed away his widow Kathy asked me to collect all his papers and tapes. With the gracious help of a small grant from the Otto Bremer Foundation I was able to do that. Those materials include every article, essay, editorial or other public writing of his that we could find, along with video and audio taped interviews. There are also manuscripts of published and unpublished books he wrote, and a well done video documentary called, "Your Humble Serpent" by his good friend Gary Rhine, Kifaru Productions, 1995. All of this material was presented by the family to the National Museum of the American Indian where it is available to the public. A copy of this material should also be available at Little Priest Tribal College in Winnebago, Nebraska.

Hold the Turtle at a 45

One day in the late summer of 1998 I got a call from an Indian tribe seeking my help. It had recently come to light that for several years some folks in the tribe's Finance Department had been doling out "payroll advances" to a couple dozen tribal employees, including themselves. These amounts were never deducted from the employees' subsequent paychecks, nor were any other methods of repayment used.

An investigation had determined that some employees had received a few hundred dollars this way and that others had received tens of thousands of dollars, in at least one case over a hundred grand. When the results of the investigation began to hit the news, things started happening in a hurry. This was a small tribe with very limited resources and it relied heavily on grants and contracts from the federal and state governments and various foundations.

As the scope and pattern of the problem emerged, all those funding sources shut off the flow of funds, demanded audits and began insisting that monies already paid to the tribe be returned. The tribe was broke and soon worse than broke, deep in a financial hole. The tribal programs shut down, soon all the tribal employees were laid off and the tribal offices shut down. The tribe had to lay off their in-house legal counsel, and the Finance Director (among others) was under criminal investigation.

That's about the time they called me. The inquiry was

pretty straight forward: they wanted to know if I could help them with a bankruptcy. "A bankruptcy for whom?" "The whole tribal government. And we'd like to move quickly on this because when freeze-up comes this Fall the electricity will be shut off and we'll have to drain the pipes in the tribal offices." I didn't like the idea of a tribe seeking bankruptcy, but told them I'd make the 3-1/2 hour drive to the reservation to meet with the tribal leaders and a small group of volunteers who were trying to hold things together.

I've been uniquely fortunate in my career in that in over 25 years of practice I've never charged a client a dime. Indeed, that's probably why they called me. So I started going up there to the reservation once a week and staying for a couple of days at a stretch. A very fine woman innkeeper in a nearby town, being sympathetic to the circumstances, offered me a room at half price for whenever I needed it – even in the winter when the inn was closed. There was a small, committed group of volunteers who dedicated themselves to trying to sort out the books and restore some basis of credibility to their accounting. These were mostly all tribal people, but also included a retired local school superintendent who rolled up his sleeves and spent hundreds of hours there with a calculator, a phone and a good sense of humor.

The FBI showed up with a court order and a van and carted off boxes and boxes of documents. Meanwhile, I learned that the tribe had an insurance policy with a major company. The policy covered theft, but it didn't cover mismanagement. Which was this? The insurance company said mismanagement, citing a number of internal memos written over the years telling the Finance Department and the employees that this practice of giving out "payroll advances" with no plan of recoupment had to stop. I argued that it was theft, citing the FBI's criminal investigation and pending indictments. The distinction was critical. There were valid arguments on both sides and the outcome of this legal debate would determine whether the tribe got nothing, or whether they'd receive a substantial insurance settlement which would allow them to pay off some creditors and re-open some tribal programs.

I discovered that this insurance company also had policies with numerous other Indian tribes. I told them that if they wouldn't step in to help out this poor struggling tribe the moccasin telegraph would quickly spread the news and they were likely to lose their other tribal clients. I was working with a small committee of tribal leaders and the insurance company sent their lawyers over from St. Paul to meet with us a few times. They were sorry for our plight, but in their legal assessment this was not a covered problem and they were advising the insurance company not to pay.

I figured the insurance company and their attorneys were also scrutinizing this little volunteer committee and me with my little nonprofit law firm. It looked like we were going into litigation to determine whether the insurance company had an obligation to pay the tribe something for their loss. I had a hunch the insurance company had calculated that we didn't have the horses to fight them and we'd either fold and give up or be out-gunned in a blizzard of legal paper wars and depositions.

So I called my friend Brian Pierson, an attorney with a major law firm in Milwaukee. Brian had successfully litigated a high profile Indian civil rights case in federal court in Wisconsin a few years previously and thus had earned a reputation as a strong and persuasive litigator. After listening to the whole story and doing a little research himself, Brian, bless his heart, agreed to write me a letter in which he essentially pledged that if the matter went to litigation he'd step in and co-counsel it with me. I made sure the lawyers for the insurance company got a copy of that letter.

By Spring the insurance company was talking settlement possibilities. The tribe was still shut down and in desperate need of cash to pay off some debts we'd negotiated down, and to rejuvenate some basic tribal government services. At this point no one on our committee wanted lengthy and risky litigation. So we reached a tentative agreement with the insurance company whereby the tribe would get hundreds of thousands of dollars immediately upon signing a settlement agreement. Some folks thought we should hold out for more or risk an all-or-nothing decision in the courts. Others were surprised we would get anything. The tribal survival committee had balanced the factors and reached this tentative negotiated agreement with the insurance company and set a date for a final meeting to hammer out the details and hopefully get everyone to sign.

The meeting was set for 11 am on a Tuesday at the tribal offices. The insurance company was sending a team of its lawyers and negotiators, and the tribe was sending its leadership and representatives from our committee. I woke up early at home, put on my best (only) dark suit and a power tie and headed out for the reservation. This was my meeting. This was potentially our major accomplishment since the original request to file bankruptcy. This could be the tipping point.

It was a cool Spring morning in the Great North Woods and there was not much traffic on the two lane highways. About here I should mention that I brake for turtles, and I help them across the road. About three hours into the drive, there in the middle of the road at the bottom of the hill in front of me was a turtle. I pulled up and stopped on the shoulder. The turtle was likely older than I was and huge. It was a Snapping Turtle almost 18" in diameter.

Not wanting to get fiercely bit for my trouble, I walked

around behind it and picked it up and, as is my practice, I carried it toward the ditch in the direction it was heading. About the time I got to the shoulder of the road holding this heavy turtle out in front of me, it let go a forceful spray of liquid all over my shirt, jacket and pants. It seemed like a quart, it must've been a pint.

I drove the last 45 minutes to the meeting with the windows open, the heater and fan on full blast and part of the time I even had the car door propped open with my knee. It all helped, but I was still pretty damp when I got there. Fortunately it was a dark suit. All the way I'd struggled with how to make my entrance. There was a lot riding on this deal for my client. A lot depended on our perceived attitude and our confidence. I decided I really didn't want to walk in there and try to explain what was on me. (Fortunately it didn't smell much.)

So after rehearsing it in my mind in the windy wet car ride, I strode into the room clutching my briefcase to my belly, said good morning and made a friendly joke about someone in the room to whom all eyes quickly turned as I sat down and scooted my chair up close to the table.

The meeting went well, the deal was done, and the check was issued on the spot. But the next time I carry a turtle I'm going to hold it at a 45 degree angle.

An Illegal Vacation

*O*ne day in the spring of 2005 I got an email from my son Tenzin. He was living in Costa Rica and had to periodically leave the country to renew his visa. He said he was bored with taking the bus to Guatemala, so how about a little adventure? I said, "What you got in mind?" He said, "How about meeting in Havana?"

How many dads get an invitation like that? I quickly said yes and we started looking for dates and tickets. During that search I learned that Bush Jr. had ratcheted up the U.S. embargo of Cuba, making travel there by U.S. citizens a more serious or seriously enforced crime, and eliminating, for the most part, the "education" visas that were fairly easy to get under Clinton. I was warned it was a penalty of up to ten years in prison and/or up to $25,000 in fines. It's a felony offense.

That was a sobering discovery for someone whose livelihood is based on a professional license that would likely be revoked for a conviction of a federal felony. I also discovered that the Center for Constitutional Rights provided assistance if you are busted, and unless you're engaged in political activity, there's a good chance of getting the whole thing substantially reduced... whatever that means. The next thing I learned was that those U.S. citizens wanting to go to Cuba could do so by flying from either Canada or Mexico, being careful to book separate tickets - not connecting tickets with a U.S. based flight. This didn't make it legal, it just made it possible.

I weighed all the factors and risks and then went with my gut. There was no way in hell I was going to let some bullshit archaic U.S. foreign policy stop such a unique father-son adventure. I wasn't about to re-contact my son and say, "Sorry son, President Bush doesn't think we should do this." And so the clandestine planning began. It was easy for Tenzin, he just flew into Havana from Costa Rica, no muss, no fuss, just be sure to not get a Cuban stamp in your passport. Since neither the Costa Ricans nor the Cubans respected Bush, that wasn't a problem.

For me it was a bit trickier. The idea being to leave no tracks, no paper trail. I found out there were daily flights from Cancun to Havana and figured out how to get a ticket for cash. Then I found a destination airline that flew about 250 people from Minneapolis to Cancun every Saturday morning and flew them back the next following Sunday, 9 days later. I bought a ticket. Krista bought me a Mayan print shirt and I went to the Minneapolis airport and joined my fellow 250 party revellers waiting for their fun-filled week in Cancun.

When the plane landed in Cancun and my plane mates went out the main terminal's front doors to head for the big buses to the beach hotels, I went out a side door and walked across the tarmac to a smaller terminal, where I paid cash for a round trip ticket to Havana. Tenzin and I met at the Havana airport, changed money (this was a cash trip, no tracks) and caught a cab to a moderately priced hotel downtown. Just to show how much we were <u>not</u> engaged in political activities, we didn't realize until we got there that the very next day, May Day, was Fidel's famous annual multi-hour speech to a million people gathered in a massive open space in Havana about a mile from our hotel.

What the hell, when in Rome...eh? So the next morning we walked to the site of the speech. The closer we got the more people were going the same way. Finally we got there, someone was speaking before Fidel, and it was broadcast over dozens of speakers spread throughout the sea of people. We stayed for the beginning of Fidel's speech. But it was hot in the sun, it was crowded, it was hard to understand and we remembered there was a TV in the bar in the hotel. It was a certainty Fidel's speech would be on. We caught a bicycle rickshaw that sat two passengers and our driver started pedaling us back. As we were going along, he called over his shoulder to us, "Where are you from?" We said we were from the States. He stopped peddling, turned and looked at us and asked if we were criminals. We said no. He said, "Well, you are now."

It was a great week. Much is written about Cuba so no need to here. Just a few observations:

- When you get out in the country on the highways you discover there are hitchhiking police. It's their job to make sure that if you're driving a state owned vehicle (which 90% of the vehicles are) you stop and pick up hitchhikers. It's the law.
- The whole world is there enjoying Cuba – except for those with U.S. passports.
- It's true that music, art, good food and romance are abundant in Cuba.
- If you owned a private car before the Revolution, you can still have that private car – if you can keep it running. So your '54 Ford may now have more bondo than metal for body, and you may be sitting on a Russian truck seat inside, but it's still your '54 Ford and it's yours.
- Lots of things are broken in Cuba, and most folks are engaged in some form of underground economy. For instance, we stayed in rooms in private homes where the folks who lived there were happy for the extra cash income.
- Health care is free. But if you want the best, and

you want it now, you better come bearing gifts.

· We left a book of Gary Snyder's poems and essays in the backseat of a '54 Ford taxi in a small farming town in the middle of the island.

The trip out of there was much like coming in. I asked the Cuban customs agent not to stamp my passport. He looked at me and said, "Ah, yes, American." But when I landed in Cancun going through Mexican customs and asked the agent not to stamp my passport, he asked why he shouldn't. I said because I'm American. He asked again why he shouldn't. I slipped him a ten dollar bill; he smiled and brought down his stamp hard. I looked and he had stamped his desk top, an inch from my passport. He smiled and gave my passport back to me.

Well, time to rejoin my fellow Cancun revellers. I walked across the tarmac to the main terminal, went into a men's room and put on the nice Mayan print shirt I'd been saving, and walked to our gate area. Some of the folks gathered there for our return flight remembered me from the flight down the week before. They said they hadn't seen me around all week, and did I have a good time? I smiled and assured them I had a great time.

On Returning From a Felonious Trip to Cuba

How furthering it is to see
The good the bad and the ugly
How hindering it is to be
Prohibited from doing so.

Down the Mississippi on a Glorified Raft

Maybe it was the adventurous heart of adolescence. Maybe it was the writing genius of Mark Twain. Whatever it was, when I first read Huckleberry Finn I was hooked on a dream. I felt that book in my heart and bones. I got what it was about and my young spirit was along for the ride, lazing on that raft and helping tie up to the shore in the dark.

I loved that story but figured floating down the Mississippi River on a raft was just a metaphor for me. Then in my late teens when I learned how accessible the world was I thought about it again as "maybe some day." Then when I was 30 years old in law school one of my professors, Jeremy Davis, told me he'd done it the previous year on a sailboat with a few of his buddies. The dream was rekindled. After that I thought of it as "some day I want to." And it stayed like that for the next 20 plus years.

Then one evening around a fire in northern Wisconsin I mentioned this idea to two friends from South Africa, Sean Penrith and Bobby Buchanan. They immediately took to it as a quintessentially American adventure, and one they'd like to have while they were living here. Sean had sailed the seas on a two-man sailboat. He's an intrepid organizer, energetic and engaged. Bobby is an incredibly talented quiet man with unusually savvy practical skills and understanding of how things work. He's one of those guys who, when you're embarking on an uncharted adventure requiring a cool head and resourcefulness, if he's available a voice in your head says, "Don't leave home without him." These are two gutsy guys.

Thereafter we kicked the notion around periodically around the fires in my yard or when we'd meet at a party. There was an eager enthusiasm tempered by a tentative wondering about each other's level of commitment . . . as well as one's own. Anybody can get excited about such a trip over a few beers. Lots of friends said they wanted to go when they'd hear us talking about it, and that complicated the equation as well.

As luck would have it, it turned out Tenzin was going to be around during the next year and was "absolutely" interested. That was the tipping point. When it occurred to me that I could actually float down the Mississippi with my son among a good solid crew of four, the whole thing started to look more real.

Early in '05 we had our Come to Jesus meeting at our kitchen table. Sean, the organizer, had the pen, paper and calculator. We roughed out the cost and the duration, figuring if we shoved off in LaCrosse, Wisconsin we could make it to New Orleans in two weeks and the whole trip should cost about a grand a piece. There was beer at the table.

The South Africans lived along the Wisconsin River and had an old aluminum pontoon boat with a new wooden deck they'd put on it. I had a 50 hp Honda four-stroke outboard motor in good running condition. We determined, rightly as it turned out, that we'd make a good crew of traveling companions with enough similar and complimentary skills, interests and attitudes that the whole thing could work. By the end of the evening we'd shaken hands on the deal, agreed to pool some money for start up costs and selected Sean as treasurer. Tenzin of course was young, footloose and broke. But I was so stoked with the idea of doing this trip with him that I pledged to cover his fourth of the expenses and he agreed to contribute some extra sweat equity and bring a video camera.

While Sean and I started collecting maps and accounts of other's Mississippi River adventures, Bobby took charge of the most important part: tricking out the pontoon to make it ready for the big river. Structurally, we figured we needed a roof. It had to be lightweight, but substantial enough to hold our weight and our gear and weather waves and storms. The roof would give us essential shade and keep us relatively dry in the rain. Bobby ordered aluminum tubing and extruded pieces for corners and fittings. The guy is good. His design and planning were damn near flawless and that roof still sits solidly on that pontoon to this very day.

We all pitched in to put it together over many weeks, and rigged up lighting, a built-in radio, and a ladder to the upper deck off the stern. We had two bag chairs for the front of the deck and a couple for midships around a little table. We hung a gas lantern from the roof in the interior near the steering console and right over an old gas grill. There were two hammocks hung, one along either side, which proved very popular. And there was a kayak strapped along one side and a bicycle on the other. Both were outside the deck of the boat. We used them both during the course of the trip, but neither very much. There were two large coolers, one for food and one for beer, and four five-gallon gas cans housed in a wooden box on the stern. There was a 30" high aluminum wall framing the deck except for a three feet deep patio on the bow where the two chairs sat exposed to the River. On the side doors in this low wall was emblazoned the name of this good ship, "Sunbird."

Thanks primarily to Bobby's engineering and fabrication skills we eventually got the Sunbird seaworthy. Meanwhile, we were collecting and studying some good navigational maps for the northern half of the River and reading about the system of locks that the Corp of Engineers placed in the River to allow big ship and barge traffic to make the trip without encountering shallow water, rapids and uncontrolled fluctuations.

After what we thought at the time were reasonable calculations we determined that if we set out from LaCrosse, Wisconsin, we could make it to New Orleans in two weeks and pass through 19 of the 27 locks (the other eight being upstream from LaCrosse). We were right about the locks.

The day before the launch we put the Sunbird on a trailer and a dozen of our friends and relatives accompanied us in a caravan from Wausau to LaCrosse where we pitched camp in a park along the shore and put the boat in the water. After a festive night we finished outfitting and loading the Sunbird and shoved off mid morning on a sunny August day.

The Fits and Starts of a Ready Crew

Only took us three years to find the time
'til we (thank you Bobby) rigged the old pontoon
the Good Ship Sunbird
and it was got together
good as we could do
under our circumstances ... you understand
pesky day jobs
(wonderful) women
a wild hair here and there

At first we were worried
we weren't prepared
we'd left something out
we'd get out there and gone
couldn't put a finger on it
we took a risk
shoved off

beyond reach of what's behind
fates to the wind
and later that day
when the boat gained a rhythm
we opened the bag chairs
and there they were –
cup holders.

All was well for awhile.

You wouldn't think you could get lost on a river, but within a half an hour we couldn't find the main channel. Turns out there are a lot of islands and marshy bays in that part of the River and not all the passages are navigable. We wandered around and ran aground, and had to back out of some too shallow channels. Eventually we found our way out into the wonderland of the Upper Mississippi. There were boats of every size and description out there, going both upstream and down. Large expensive yachts, fishing boats, speedboats pulling skiers, and of course tugs pushing barges. But there was only one funky tricked out pontoon with a roof and a couple guys swaying in bright colored hammocks.

A lot has been written about the treacherous waters of the Mississippi. I haven't read most of it, but I can tell you at least some of it's true. The main channel is marked with red and green buoys, and as long as you stay left of green and right of red you won't run aground. But that's about the only thing you can know for sure. A big yacht throws a lot of wake. Being passed between two big yachts going in opposite directions creates some chaotic and even thrilling wake. All of which is magnified exponentially if you replace the yachts with barges.

The barge traffic is a central feature of the Mississippi River experience. Each barge itself is a big rusty steel flat bottomed vessel about 45' wide and 200' long. They're typically lashed tightly together with heavy, rusty steel cable. A fleet of these lashed together barges might be two, three, four or five barges wide, and it might be from two to seven barges long. That's a lot of water displacement. Then consider that these barges might all be empty, in which case they're riding high and moving fast. Or they might be full of coal, grain, rocks, scrap metal, ocean size containers, who knows what; in which case they're riding low, going slow and pushing a lot of wake water. Now consider that those enormous wakes (sometimes so big and rolling you can barely tell they're waves) have so much mass and momentum that not only do they push out from the barges, but they hit the shore and bounce back out across the river back in the opposite direction. Mix all that up with the wakes of other crafts out there and you can begin to understand how early that first afternoon we did our first bow stall.

A bow stall occurs when you get caught up in the wakes in such a way that the bow of the pontoon goes down in a trough and gets buried in a giant wave rolling by, which pushes the stern up in the air so that the motor is screaming totally out of the water and the gas lantern swings up slamming into the ceiling. If you happen to be out on the bow patio at the time you'll be lucky if all you get is soaked.

These massive fleets of lashed together barges are pushed by a tug boat. Today's tug boats are jet propelled. Like an airplane jet pushes huge quantities of air at high speed, a tug does something similar with water. One side effect that affected us is that the force of the jets down into the water rips the vegetation on the bottom out by the roots. The displaced vegetation can be so thick it mucks up the propeller on our little raft and we have to shut down, tip the motor up and clean off the weeds from the prop.

Upper Mississippi

Main Street looks different from the river
The riverfront looks different from the river
Towns and cities too
The river looks different from the river.

The hum of the motor back in the well
Long line of mindless barges with their determined
tugs
Churning the water deeply
Ripping up the grasses
That bind our little motor down
Whirlpools and schools of whirlpools
Linger and spin the trailing tail
Of slow motion barges
Industrial dinosaurs

Flat boats john boats keel boats steamers
Floating casinos not moving at all
Ghostly in the morning mist
Speed boats house boats launches pontoons
Jet skis yachts cabin cruisers
Riding each others wake
On the Upper Mississippi.

Little towns strung along the shoreline
Maybe a broke down gas pier
Maybe a funky little harbor
The houses face the river
As a sign of respect
For this big wet vein
Whose watershed extends over 28 states.

Barges heaped with coal coming up
Barges binned with grain going down

Artery, vein
Some kind of energy exchange.

And so it goes till you come to a lock. The locks are staffed by crews of people who live locally. Some of them are friendly and funny, some of them decidedly not so. When the lock system was being developed some principled souls determined that since it was our birthright to flow freely on our navigable rivers, just because the Corps put a lock in there doesn't mean it shouldn't still be free.

A lock is part of a dam that goes all the way across a river. It has massive hydraulic doors on both ends. The water below the dam/lock is lower than that above. If you're coming from upstream going down, the downstream door on the lock is closed and the upstream door opened until the water in the lock is filled to the same level as the upstream river. You then drive your boat into the lock and the upstream door closes behind you. Once it's closed (they're very nearly watertight) water is slowly let out the downstream side until the water inside (and your boat) are at the downstream water level. The lower gate is then opened and you motor on out into the open river again.

There are, of course, some protocols involved. One I like a lot is the general rule that it's 'first come first served.' This means that if our little pontoon going downstream gets to a lock before a mammoth barge with millions in cargo gets to it coming upstream, the lock serves us first. I'm sure there are some exceptions and nuances, but the rule held pretty true for us. What? How big are they? Oh, think of a lock as about the size of a football field. The vertical drop in each lock varied from maybe only six feet of difference to as much as over 30'.

As you talk to the Lockmasters (the friendly ones) you quickly learn that they've seen pretty much everything that floats go through. Everything from a couple guys on a tiny raft lashed to two 50-gallon drums to barge fleets so huge they have to be taken through the lock in sections and re-assembled on the other side.

Waving

It's a weekday work day morning
Mostly just the serious river runners
Out here now

And they mostly follow the custom
International custom
Of acknowledging those you pass
In other vessels
A little wave
A nod or doff of hat
Maybe just fingers to the brim
A sweep of arm or one finger wave
International acknowledgement
On the high seas
On Old Man River
On the gravel roads of the Dakotas

People who would argue
Maybe even fight
If they got any closer in time or space
Don't agree on nothin'
But this international acknowledgement
The custom of a wave

In the Upper (which mean north of St. Louis) there's traffic out there and settlements near the shore. Importantly, there are marinas. Some fairly elaborate where you can berth your boat, and get not only gas but a meal and a shower. Others are just a dock and a shack and nothing much besides gas. What allows for these riverside accommodations and variety of boats and activities on the Upper is the system of locks. They make this wild and powerful River somewhat manageable and predictable. You could think of it as giant river-shaped lakes between each set of locks, but with a serious current.

The Upper at Dusk

Houses on the hillsides
Houses on the top
Houses on the river
That never stops

Red light green light
Passing port to port
Ships in the twilight
Staying on course

At night we tried a variety of things. Out of respect for the multitude of powerful and potentially deadly dangers on this great river we determined to stop each day before dark. A couple nights early in the trip we tied up at marinas, simply because they were there as we were going by late in the afternoon. On those nights, like all the others, we slept outside on or near the boat. We pitched a tent on the roof of the boat. We pitched tents on the shore or on islands. We slept in the hammocks. We cooked dinner on a two-burner Coleman stove or an open fire. We got relentlessly attacked by millions of mosquitoes that would arrive out of nowhere in a matter of minutes at dusk and not leave till morning.

Speaking of the Coleman stove, we had to ditch the gas grill. It was Bobby's idea and a good one. We all noticed that we were going a little slower down river than we thought we would. And the motor seemed to be working a little harder than we hoped it would. One day Bobby announced we had to get rid of two things to lighten our load enough to, by his reckoning, make an appreciable difference. We had a five-gallon can of bad gas that had given us trouble the day before and was now just sitting idle. Bobby said that can of gas and the grill had to go. Just replacing the gas with clean gas wouldn't help the problem he was working on, which he deemed more serious than the factor of having an extra five gallons of gas on board. So at the next stop there was a funky old marine mechanic who said he'd be happy to have the gas can and bad gas, and would give away the grill to some of the guys working on the barges, they'd be happy to have it for cooking on the water.

Sure enough, with those two items gone from the stern area all of a sudden the boat stood up a little higher in the water and planed out as it should, giving us better speed and gas mileage and a quieter ride.

For the most part it was mellow days, cruising along through new territory every moment. There was enough of a risk out there to keep a nice little edge on the trip all the time. There was enough room to walk around a little on the Sunbird. Sean was busy keeping a daily blog going chronicling the trip, which it turns out was being closely followed back home and beyond. Tenzin kept looking for cell phone power so he could challenge his own better judgment by talking endlessly with a young lady back home who brought him grief, trouble and down as near as I could tell. Bobby just liked to drive. Although we took turns pretty well at most everything there was an unsaid recognition that driving the boat had some special value for him. You could sit on a chair on the patio bow with a coffee or a beer and be right on the front edge of the journey right where the boat cut the water. You could go up on the roof to get fully away and enjoy a little different view. There was lots of good napping, daydreaming and book reading that went on in those hammocks through the days. It was truly a memorable way to travel through the country.

Why We're Here

Sean was busy at his laptop. After his third quick move to avoid splash when we crossed a wake he said, "Shite, it's hard to get any work done." To which I responded, "That's why I'm here." Bobby added a deep chuckling grin and thumbs up.

The Upper was by far more interesting than the lower. I was reading, "Life on the Mississippi" on the trip and was somehow relieved Mark Twain wasn't around to see what had happened to his beloved river. In that book he laments the encroaching modernity of his time wherein locals would go out and put lanterns on the riverbank to mark a change of course or a growing sandbar. Twain was so enamored of the incredible skillfulness of the riverboat pilots that he found it a dumming down of their skills to do such things. Twain found such modern local town actions to be an insult to the river memory and intuition of those fine pilots of his era. Oh, if he only knew.

Once you get past the last of the 27 locks, below where the Missouri and the Ohio have come in, you get the feeling you're on an industrial channel. . . a channel characterized by commerce and fear. There are no more marinas. There are no more visible towns. There is no more variety of boats out there. There's nowhere to get gas or food. There's nowhere even to tie up your boat.

The Mississippi has a storied history of havoc – jumping its banks, shifting its channels, carrying away what folks have valued. But what we have done in return is far more tragic to me. The Lower is, at least as far down as Memphis and likely beyond, a great big ugly canal used by barges. The Corps has rip rapped virtually the entire bank on both sides. It's just a uniform gravel embankment at a uniform angle with a uniform height. And the towns? Well, the towns on the Lower have all turned their backs on the river - and worse. Often you can't even see them from the water. Some of them have moved totally to the other side of the riprapped levy and unless you spot the top of the town's water tower you'd never know there was a town there – a town along the Mississippi invisible from the water! The towns you can spot you can spot by the presence of a fortress like concrete wall replacing the riprap. Maybe there's some graffiti on the river side of the wall, but that's about it.

With the river so pushy due to channelization and nowhere to dock, it's a real challenge to stop anywhere. When we got low on gas and spotted the top of a water tower where the map showed a town we had to be quick and skilful to stop - the current so fast, no bays, no trees. We'd put one guy on each of the front corners of the boat each holding an anchor that was tied by a long rope to the stern. We'd drive the boat bow first into the gravel bank to hopefully get the pontoons to dig in a little. Meanwhile, the instant we crunched into the shore the two guys would jump on land and run straight to either side as far as the anchor lines would allow and jam the anchors into the ground. This, when it worked, gave us a four point landing – the two pontoon tips and the anchors out at about 45 degrees.

Then we'd have to slog those gas cans up over the levy and into town to look for gas. Sometimes we had to call a cab to get gas for the boat. How out of whack is that in a river town?

Bats on the Mississippi

Early evening light
A wave of bats

Near a half mile long at times
Undulating cohesively
Over the river
Rolling as a fast wave
Thick and connected thousands

Suddenly they split in the middle
And half of this wave veers off to the left
Making its' own swoop off the river
Low over the east shore trees
The other half of this quick elastic wave
Dives down out of sight behind an island
And poof
It's over

Unless you could read
The history of the air
You'd never know what happened.

One time on the Lower we spotted what appeared to be a sandbar. It was outside the red and green buoys marking the navigable channel, and appeared to have a lee side where we hoped to tie up easily and out of the wake of the giant barges. We ran the pontoons gently into the sandbar and Tenzin jumped off the bow to plant an anchor. But he planted himself. Turns out it was pure muck and he sunk in up to his thighs. It was just downright unfriendly out there on the Lower. It's pretty bad when you have a whole river shore to yourself and can't find a place to sleep. If Mark Twain wasn't already dead I think the scene out there would kill him.

The barges on the Lower were sometimes the biggest we'd seen. I remember one lashed together flotilla of 35 of those giant things. Five across and seven long, all hauling something. One time there was a bunch of barges being pushed by a tug which gave us a sight most folks don't ever see. All these barges were heaped with coal, but one of them was on fire. We could see this dark smoke off in the distance and when we caught up to it, sure enough, this heaping barge full of coal, still being pushed down the River, was on fire. We couldn't see flames but there was a lot of smoke. Wonder how it started. Wonder how they dealt with it.

Barge Wake on the Lower Mississippi

"You take about 35 empty barges and a big tug going upstream on the Lower and you got yourself a phenomenon."

This is the stuff into which
Bobby did a bow stall.
The initial waves are big slow rollers
Then you meet the churn
Spinning off the four foot rolling holes
Following the stern
About then run into waves returning
From shore
Having ricocheted off both banks
They cross through each other
And in so doing make waves out of wake
That break straight up
On the surface
While underneath the cross currents
Meld momentum and move on
With giant slow motion.

When the biggest wave breaks over our bow
The tug and barges are a mile away.

The Mississippi River water does not appear healthy. As you'd expect, the further south you go the truer this becomes. By the time the Missouri, the Ohio and many other rivers have merged into it, it has murky clouds of various shades of color and clarity that sort of blur into one another but don't quite become homogenous, in spite of the many whirlpools that appear on the swift surface. And the water temperature when we went downstream in August was in the mid to high 80's. We didn't eat anything that came out of the river; didn't even feel safe bathing in it. What a sorrowful commentary on the major artery of this country.

That's not to say there isn't life out there. Although many indigenous species are no longer seen, one alien species got our full attention. After many days on the water we were rolling along one afternoon when Tenzin saw a fish jump. That was rare, especially south of the locks, and then Bobby said, "There's another one." This was enough to get Sean to look up from his blogging machine and pretty soon we saw a few more; then quite a few more and before long they were jumping all around the boat like popcorn. Altogether we saw hundreds, and some of them were big, maybe 20 pounds and jumping up to six feet out of the water.

You hear fishermen talk about how the fishing was so good they were practically jumping into the boat. But this ain't no fisherman's tale. They were literally jumping into our boat and fortunately Tenzin captured it on video. We ran into these schools a few times and altogether 11 fish jumped onto our boat, the biggest one close to 20 pounds. There would've been 12, but one hit Bobby in the chest and bounced off back into the water.

After days and days of nothing but the same four men in a boat going a little stir crazy, having fish jumping like popcorn and onto the boat was no small event. The laughter verged on hysterical.

You Can't Make This Stuff Up

Yesterday a fish jumped onto our boat
We were several seconds stunned
As no doubt was the fish
Then we hooted and laughed
At the two pound flying carp
Because it was the stuff
Of impossible tales
Generations of fish stories
Flopping around on the deck
Like we've never seen before
Nor likely hence

A few hours later
Turning East to
Run up the Kaskaskia
All of a sudden
Whoosh here comes another one
Right through the open door
On the front of the pontoon.
We whooped and hollered
Someone mentioned dying and
Going to heaven
The improbability more
Than we could really assess

And then this afternoon
Just after the Ohio joined in
While the waters were roiling
As the two mighty rivers sorted out
Their new and irrevocable touch
No more than a couple miles downstream
Some bigger fish started jumping
Alongside the boat
They'd jump a few feet in the air
Then hit the water only to jump again

Sometimes skipping three or four times like a stone
And we were jazzed by it all
Pointing and yelling out
So as a joke
I got up with a grin
Went and opened the bow door
And before I could get back to my chair
This 25 pound flying carp
Landed on the front deck and came
Flipping and thrashing through the door
All the way back to Tenzin at the wheel
Trailing blood and scales
And I remember thinking
Wait a minute that was supposed to be a joke
I tell you
You can't make this shit up.

Then toward evening
Pulling into Hickman Harbor, Kentucky
Motoring slow toward town
Six more fish jumped onto the boat
For a total of nine.
It would've been ten but one bounced
Off Bobby's chest
And landed back in the water.
You can't make this stuff up.

(I'd add that the next morning another fish came six feet out of the water and over our side rails, just missing Sean's open laptop and thumped down in our stern... but I don't want to stretch my credibility beyond what the uninitiated can believe.)

Unfortunately, the flying fish story goes beyond our simple enjoyment. Folks on the river said they were Asian Flying Carp, an alien species from far away with no natural predators and voracious appetites that are one way or another decimating natural species and bio-relationships in our fresh waters. There is a great concern that the fish that flew past us are heading into our whole network of rivers and into the Great Lakes.

There have been a couple of clues in this story that we didn't make it all the way to New Orleans. Such is the case. Turns out we miscalculated the distance by about a thousand river miles. Way back in the planning phase of this adventure Sean found, ordered and received a thick book of great maps from the U.S. Army Corps of Engineers entitled "Upper Mississippi River Navigation Charts." Those detailed charts had everything we'd need for navigation – everything except the Lower Mississippi.

Apparently, they were out of paper navigation charts for the Lower, but did have them on computer discs. Sean, always keen to do anything with computers, got the Lower on discs, but we never studied them. I can't pinpoint the exact moment we went astray in our calculations of the River's length and the time it would take us to run it. But I can say this: that oversight was the genius of the trip. If we would have planned more carefully and over-thought all the elements of the trip, we would've figured out more precisely what we were getting into and never would've done it.

Everybody had two weeks for this trip, plus a couple of travel days on each end. But, in fact, the trip we planned with the boat we had is a three-week trip on the water. Once we realized this we called back home and had our friend Joe, and his girlfriend Diamond, bring my car and a pontoon trailer down to meet us in Memphis. And thus it was we ended the trip in Memphis with a couple days and nights of barbeque and blues and long hot showers before heading home.

As it turns out that miscalculation was perhaps fortuitous. Had we continued down the Mississippi at our pace we would've arrived in New Orleans at the same time as Hurricane Katrina.

The Belly Button of the World

*O*n October 20, 2010 the first international conference on peyote convened at UAEM State University in Toluca, Mexico. It was hosted by the University's Anthropology Department and its formal title was "The International Congress on Traditional Medicine and Public Health: Peyote, Traditional Medicine or Recreational Drug?" The title was a bit misleading in that the conference focused almost exclusively on the medicinal or sacramental use of peyote, with only an occasional disparaging reference to other uses. There were three full days of presentations and panel discussions. Nearly every session in the Anthropology Department's lecture bowl was packed. A mixture of scholars, practitioners, health professionals, students and others filled the seats, sat in the aisles and stood shoulder to shoulder in the back of the room. The presentations included medical research, scholarly reports, personal stories, anthropological and legal discussions. One of the keynote presentations was by Dr. John Halpern, a Harvard psychiatrist whose now famous study shows that there are no negative effects to motor skills or cognition from long term use of peyote when it is used in the ritual and ceremonial contexts of indigenous practitioners, specifically in this study members of the Native American Church.

As an adjunct to the central theme of peyote, there were also presentations on the ritual and healing uses of ayahuasca, a tea from Brazil with psychotropic properties somewhat similar to peyote. Similar to Dr. Halpern's report on peyote use, Dr. Josep Maria Fabregas, a psychiatrist from Spain, reported positive results from his study of ayahuasca when used in proper context for spiritual and/ or healing purposes.

Meanwhile, while these presentations were going on inside, out in the courtyard there was a bustling scene of vendors with arts, crafts, healing supplies and food. There were Huichol curanderos, colorful Aztec dancers with big drumbeats, and many sidebar conversations.

One of the sidebar conversations was an important talking circle convened in a glass-walled room overlooking the courtyard and on the roof of a University cafe. In this circle were indigenous practitioners of peyote ways from Mexico, the U.S. and Canada. Although convened off the formal agenda, this meeting fulfilled one of the central purposes of the Congress. In this talking circle representatives of various peyote traditions introduced themselves to each other and discussed issues of mutual concern – particularly how they could help each other to protect their holy sacrament and preserve their ways of life.

From the Mexican side was heard the concern about a proposed silver mining operation right in the sacred peyote country of northern Mexico and the lack of indigenous control over that area. Also raised was the need for organization among the various peyote people in Mexico who lack the kind of legal identity found in the U.S. and Canada. To these concerns the peyote people from the north offered to share litigation expertise and strategies from similar recent and ongoing cases in the U.S. where giant corporations were threatening sacred Native ground. The northerners also offered to help with organizing, such as incorporation as a religious organization as has been done for many years in the U.S. and Canada, but has yet to occur in Mexico.

The peyote people from the U.S. and Canada representing various branches of the Native American Church spoke of their concern over diminishing amounts of peyote available in the U.S. (ten percent of peyote grows in the U.S. and ninety percent in Mexico). A combination of factors: the growth of the NAC, a long-term drought trend in Texas where the peyote grows, and the diminishing amount of land available to harvest peyote, all combine to create a growing problem of supply and price in the U.S.

To this concern the Mexican peyote people offered that perhaps a way could be found to gather peyote, in a sustainable way, from some areas of Mexico and send it north.

These problems and potential solutions were discussed in a respectful and understanding way. Various possibilities and scenarios were explored in some detail, and contact information was exchanged.

Another sidebar conversation of note occurred one evening in a classroom. This brought together the lawyers from Mexico, the U.S. and Canada to discuss legal hurdles and options. The conversation focused primarily on how to protect peyote in Mexico and give voice to the interests of the peyote people. Incorporating a peyote-based religious group was discussed, perhaps modeled somewhat on those that exist in the U.S. and Canada. But the main discussion was on choosing legal strategies. There was a well articulated perspective that championed the use of litigation to force Mexico to enforce its existing laws in a good way and compel through the courts the clarification of current legal ambiguities. This discussion was led by the clear and colorful Roy Haber, a long-time civil rights attorney who recently and successfully represented one of the ayahuasca religious groups (Santo Daime) in their effort to secure protection for their importations and use of ayahuasca in the U.S.

Another legal approach presented favored going to the Mexican federal Congress and amending the existing

laws to provide a comprehensive legal framework that protects legitimate religious use of peyote and also protects
the peyote from exploitation and diversion. This discussion was led by me as a 20-year attorney for the Native
American Church and one of the attorneys who fought successfully for similar legislation in the U.S. in the '90s. Roy
and I playfully and respectfully teased each other out on
the relative virtues of litigation versus legislation. In the
end it is left to the Mexicans to gauge which approach best
suits the circumstances of the Mexican legal and political
systems. Perhaps there is a role for both strategies.

The organizers of this International Congress on
Peyote are indicative of the complexities of this issue in
Mexico. The awful truth is that the Conquistadors and the
Catholic Church were so brutally effective at destroying
indigenous cultures in Mexico that the country was left
with considerably less recognition of Native people than
even the U.S. and Canada. The horrific destruction (beginning in the 1500's with torture techniques imported from
the Catholic-sponsored Spanish Inquisition) left very few
Native groups in this country with a surviving specific tribal identity. The Huichols are perhaps the most prominent
example of a relatively intact specific tribal identity. The
Tarahumaras and a few other groups survive recognizably,
but even these groups lack the legal status and recognition
of tribes in the U.S. and Canada. I am advised that there
are no treaties, and no land-based reservations based on
government-to-government recognition. The devastation
of these people was so severe that even today Mexican
people with significant indigenous blood will often decline
to identify themselves as such, considering it an embarrassment.

However, there is a resurgence going on. There have
remained and survived pockets of indigenous people who
do know their Native roots and histories. Some of these

Mestizos (people of mixed indigenous and Spanish blood) have done a lot of research on the cultural and spiritual traditions of their people. Based on my conversations in Mexico it seems that a significant motivation for this return to those earlier cultural and religious expressions comes from a general dissatisfaction with Christianity, particularly contemporary Christianity. Not only is it guilty of unabashed cultural genocide and massive amounts of torture and death, but for many it lacks a spiritual depth dimension, especially when it comes to individual experience. No doubt there are many and complex reasons for this resurgence.

These Mestizos are most certainly a small minority of Mexican Mestizos (which essentially are most all Mexicans). But they are serious. They are dusting off the old ways of their ancestors to the best of their ability, and they are going about it in a deliberate and respectful way. However, a lot of damage has been done over the centuries and many of the teachings and ceremonies have been lost. So these Mestizos are forming alliances with stronger contemporary Native people who have retained these things – such as the Huichols in Mexico and various spiritual practices found among the Indians of the U.S. and Canada. Prominent in this regard are the peyote traditions, rituals and teachings of the Huichols and of the Native American Church.

In furtherance of those interests, the International Congress concluded with a road trip. About 40 people boarded a chartered bus and, followed by a short caravan of smaller cars and a busload of Huichols, headed out on a 10-hour trip into the desert to an area the Huichols call "the belly button of the world."

The travelling group included the Mestizo peyote people, Huichols and NAC Roadmen and members from the U.S. and Canada. This was an all-Native travelling group with few exceptions: the psychiatrist, the lawyer, and two Spanish researchers.

There is a vast region of northern Mexico in which the peyote grows. In the heart of this region an area has been set aside by the Mexican government for the exclusive use of the Huichols in relation to peyote. But there is much peyote growing in the desert all around the outside of this set-aside area. It was to such a place that we travelled, deep into the state of San Luis de Potosi.

As our caravan approached the dusty little village from which the peyote hunt was to be launched and on the edge of which our all-night ceremonies were to occur, we passed a gas station and our leaders shouted for the bus to stop. It turned out that one of the Huichol leaders before we left Toluca had called some of his urban Mexican friends and supporters in Mexico City. He told them about this historic event that was going to occur out in the desert ... and apparently he invited them to come. Thus we found assembled in the gas station parking lot in the morning sun another caravan of vehicles carrying about another 40 people. This rag-tag bunch was variously referred to as "the neo-Huichols" and "los hippies." Our leaders convened an impromptu meeting with them in the parking lot. It was explained to them that what was about to occur was a long-planned religious ceremony honoring some specific traditions. It was described as being of historic significance and including practitioners and invited guests from the countries to the north. It was urged that los hippies kindly and out of respect not intrude and leave this event to the traditional people.

To this, los hippies responded that they thought the whole thing was a cool idea, and they were eager to participate in it. That's why they were here. They'd been invited by a Huichol leader, had driven 10 hours just like us and had every right to be wherever they wanted to be. They offered assurances that they would be unobtrusive but otherwise wouldn't budge from their intentions.

Leaving them at the gas station on the little highway we drove on and came to a final stop in the center of a dusty little town off the highway. The Huichol bus was already parked there, and a meeting was coming together in a raised gazebo in the town square. The meeting included our Mestizo leaders from the bus and numerous Huichols, along with the local "mayor" and some curious local community people.

It turns out there are currently five distinct groups of Huichols in Mexico, they have no collective central leadership, and they don't necessarily agree or get along. It seemed that several of the Huichol groups were represented in the gazebo meeting. This meeting went on for nearly two hours and was alternately animated and thoughtful. Although the gazebo was crowded, women worked their way through the crowd with incense burners wafting clouds of copal smoke intended to confer blessings, wisdom and good will.

The arguments were broad ranging, but the central points of debate, as translated, seemed to be these:
- Who should be allowed to go on the peyote hunt?
- Must a bull be sacrificed before anything further could occur?
- Would los hippies be welcome at the prayer ceremonies tonight?

After nearly two hours these agreements were reached:
- The Huichols would conduct the peyote hunt in their ritual way and all of the North Americans could come (including the lawyer and the psychiatrist) along with a few Mestizo leaders.
- Although proper prayers had been offered at

the beginning of the International Congress with the intent of evoking a blessing that would carry through the entire arc of the whole week, it was not enough. It would be necessary to sacrifice a bull for this peyote hunt and ceremony, and the designated leader of the whole organizing effort (Armando Loizaga) would have to do the sacrifice. But the sacrifice could occur in the morning at the end of the ceremony.

· Los hippies could not go on the peyote hunt but they could attend the all-night ceremony and were welcome to eat peyote there.

A caravan of a few packed cars and SUVs drove out into the desert along a two-track one-lane road and came to a stop at a place that seemed totally arbitrary, with no identifiable markings at all. After elaborate Huichol prayers and smudging with the ubiquitous copal, the roughly two dozen of us spread out about 10 meters apart and began slowly walking in the same direction, which happened to be west.

At first it seemed there was no peyote to be found – just scattered bushes and some very prickly cactus plants of various species. But then someone would find a peyote, seemingly hiding under a bush peeking out just above the surface of the earth. There were prayers, a small ritual, a careful cutting so the root would regenerate more peyote, a slight dirt covering of the exposed root and a little water sprinkled over the top. In this way the hunt began.

Whereas in the beginning we didn't find any peyote, once you found the first one and cut it properly all of a sudden you could find peyote everywhere as you walked carefully along watching out for spiky cacti and hunting for peyote. Although I suppose I was learning how to find it, it felt like the peyote was showing itself to me.

After an hour or so someone blew a conch shell and we all began heading back to where we started. There we found the Huichols gathered around a large bush I hadn't noticed before. There was a considerable amount of peyote growing under this bush and the Huichols were placing prayer objects in the bush and big full bags of peyote on the ground around the bush. A Huichol medicine man was conducting a ceremony for the successful harvest using a deer antler. One at a time we each stepped up and impaled one of the peyotes we'd found on a spike of the antler. It should be noted that while the size of the peyote varied, a typical size was about the same as a tennis ball. The medicine man, amidst wafts of copal, would chant and move the deer antler all around your body as you stood there, ending with the presentation of your peyote on the antler tip to just in front of your mouth where you were expected to bite off the whole thing, get it in your mouth without using your hands, and eat it.

Trepidatious as to the bitter taste of this medicine I chose a small peyote causing the medicine man to look startled and chuckle and offer me a bigger one. I think he felt sorry for me, assuming I was a lousy hunter and this was the best I could come up with. My embarrassment at that moment was compounded when I bit into the peyote and discovered that it was, in fact, sweet and not bitter. Quite surprised I moved off to the side and asked a Huichol how it could be that this peyote tasted so good, almost like an apple. He smiled and said it was because this peyote comes from the belly button of the world.

That evening we made our way over a dry riverbed to a place on the edge of town where a large tipi was set up just 30 feet west of a large leafless tree. Under the tree the Huichols made their altar on the ground. At about dark some kids showed up with burros laden with firewood for the Huichol Fire (the tipi firewood was already stacked and waiting). The fires were lit, with the whole thing arranged in such a way that the Roadman in the tipi looked through his fire and through the door of the tipi and across the short distance through the Huichol fire and to the Huichols sitting facing their fire and looking on through both fires at the Roadman in the tipi.

The tipi was near full. Other than an open pathway between the fires, the area all around the Huichol fire was full of people, perhaps some few more than a hundred. Off to the side under another tree was tethered a sheep which would be sacrificially offered in the morning as a typical part of a Huichol ceremony. And a little further away, tied to another tree was the bull Armando was scheduled to sacrifice in the morning as well. Both animals stood alert throughout the entire night, watching the people and the fire and listening to the drums.

Those in the tipi were expected to keep their seats through the night, the typical way of an NAC prayer ceremony. Those outside had a little more flexibility to get up and move around a little as need be. Peyote was passed periodically around the circle inside the tipi, the typical way of an NAC prayer ceremony. On the outside designated people moved through the crowd periodically with baskets containing peyote which had been sliced up (like apple slices) by Huichol women after the hunt in the later afternoon. One was free to eat this offered peyote and/or the peyote each of us who'd gone hunting had found in the afternoon. I noticed the sharing of peyote through the night, including individuals coming up to the Huichol altar and leaving one or more whole peyotes there.

The primary focal events of the night were the NAC tipi prayer ceremony where the wonderful peyote water drum carried on through the night, and the Huichol peyote ceremony involving chanting and blessings and other ritual elements I could not understand. Having these two venerable spiritual traditions happening with two fires facing each other was historic, intriguing and beautiful, and many of us had the humbling sense that we were participating in something historic which was likely to change the future.

But the night was a bit more complex than that. It turns out there is a third peyote tradition alive in Mexico. As it was explained to me it comes from an Aztec root (the Chichimaké people) and its central feature is group singing. Several times through the night, during what appeared to be a pause in the Huichol ceremony, a singer emerged near the fire with a stringed guitar-like instrument and began singing a few long songs. These were loud, robust, full-throated songs, and a large number of the people around the fire joined in, also with gusto, conveying a palpable sense of peace and love. I think I heard lyrics like "todo el mundo is uno", and the upbeat melodic choral songs were reminiscent of John Lennon's "Give Peace a Chance." These songs spread a feeling of kindness and well-being, although it was unclear to me whether the songs were ancient or modern.

But the night was even a bit more complex than that. Remember los hippies? They were clustered in groups on two sides of the fire. On one side many had put down blankets and were laying down covered up on the periphery of events. On another side they were more attentive. And several times during the night (I believe it always followed the group singing I just described above, but before the Huichols could then resume their lead in the ceremony) los hippies would commence with someone blowing on a six foot long Australian aboriginal didgeridoo while another started playing a four foot tall African-style drum. The true peyote people around the fire seemed gracious and tolerant toward these new ingredients. Peyote has a way of calmly bringing out the compassionate side of one's nature. But in discussions the next day I learned that I was not the only one who felt that the rhythms introduced by los hippies, although fine in their own right, were out of place and disruptive of this special, prayerful night.

In the morning first the sheep and then the bull were sacrificed in front of the Huichol altar. Their blood has significance for the Huichol who very seriously and reverentially applied it to their ritual implements and in some cases their faces. Also in the early morning there was the passing of a large pail of water from which everyone drank a little with a shared tin cup. This was followed by some morning food which had been prepared off-site and brought in at dawn.

It took many hours for the proceedings to wind down. Through the morning conversations were translated, ritual items were put away, the sacrificed animals were butchered off to the side, the sites of the fires were cleaned up, mothers unfolded cloths and fed tortillas to their little children who had slept through the night by their sides. Thank you's were generously offered and promises were made to gather together again with respect for the past and prayers for the future.

In the end the Huichols, the NAC delegation and the Mestizos who follow the Peyote Way all parted toward their homes with a better sense of who each other is, and of the variety of respected traditions within which peyote teaches. And all were talking about their shared responsibility to protect the peyote and the Peyote Way of Life.

In 1991 the remarkable Reuben Snake, Jr. (Winnebago) led a delegation of NAC folks and friends down to a remote area of Mexico for four successive nights of peyote ceremonies with the Huichols, Tarahumaras and Tephuan Indians. At that time there was a meeting of the minds of the carriers of these various peyote traditions. It was a conclave of mutual respect and shared vision for the challenges ahead to preserve these old and deep spiritual traditions.

This gathering together in 2010 was the closest we have come to a continuation of the meetings in '91. Will there be another formal "International Congress"? Will there be more travels back and forth across the border by the leaders of these Peyote Ways to share prayers and ideas and collaborations?

As one considers the depth and wisdom of these Peyote Ways amidst the increasingly selfish and superficial ways of the contemporary world, one can only be hopeful that such meetings continue and bring forth the heart of their prayers.

APPENDIX

Snapshots of Beginnings

1958: Near the Canadian Line

My paternal grandparents, Clay and Stella Botsford, lived in a big stucco house on a farm near Adams, North Dakota, in the wind swept prairie not far from the Canadian line. In 1958, you could take a train there from Grand Forks, where I was raised. I'd spend some summer time up there, and on Saturday my Grandma'd heat up enough water so everyone could have a bath in the big galvanized tub. Then we'd go to town for Saturday night. "Downtown" was only two blocks long so we were free to run off and do whatever we liked. In other words, we weren't that hard to find. And since everyone knew everyone else, mischief was thereby kept to a minimum.

Grandpa Clay was 11th generation Botsford in the U.S., descended from Henry Botsford who came over from England in 1639 and "acquired land from the Indians" near Milford, Connecticut.

By the way, not everyone got clean water in that galvanized tub.

1960: Gone Fishing

Some guys are lucky and get just the right uncle in their lives. I'm one of them. My uncle Einar Jondahl and his wife, Elva, had no kids. But they did have a paint and wallpaper store where they gave me my first job at age 11 as a stock boy, janitor and gopher. And most importantly they had a lake cottage an hour from town with a wooden fishing boat and a motor.

They took me with them to the lake on many a Friday evening for the weekend for several years. It was there that Uncle Einar taught me how to fish. Fishing doesn't work for everybody, but for some of us it is a great teacher. Fishing provides a context in which to slow down and pay attention to nature. And that's as important as it sounds. I've learned so much from observing all the interactions and interrelationships within nature simply by putting myself in the context of a boat on the water. Fishing has some things in common with meditation – a certain detachment and an opportunity to simply observe.

Uncle Einar taught me how to fish and how to run the boat, whether he was in it or not. To my great joy I was able to pass those teachings on to my son.

1961: Learning to Swear and Drive

My maternal grandfather Tom Dvorak and his peculiar second wife Jenny lived on a farm near Emerado, North Dakota. Since that was only 15 miles from Grand Forks, I got out there quite a bit. Grandpa Tom's folks had come over from what was then Czechoslovakia. He was relatively unschooled and you could hear his past in his voice. His brother had a polka band.

This guy was earthy. He taught my cousin and me how to drive, and by the time we were 12, we were driving his pickup on the gravel roads and tractors in the field. He bought a horse for each of us kids, too. I mean, he said it was mine, so I treated it like mine. Does that make it mine? Anyway, that added to the magic of learning to ride a horse. None of my buddies in town learned how to ride on their own horse.

Cussing was part of Grandpa Tom's vocabulary. He

didn't overuse it, but he didn't stifle it just because I was around either. I sure enjoyed learning how to swear properly from such a natural teacher. Like cussing was part of his vocabulary, smoking was part of his day. Since you could smoke pretty much anywhere in those days, there were always packs of cigs laying around on the kitchen table or the dashboard or the glove box. I started snitchin' them pretty early, but I don't think I smoked in front of him till I was about 15. There was a slop bucket under the kitchen sink at the farm. It was kind of like a compost bucket, but it was for feeding to the chickens, and sloppin' the hogs when we had them. In the winter, it was alright to pee in there at night so you didn't have to go to the outhouse.

I Always Thought It Smelled Fantastic

I always thought it smelled fantastic
when we'd first hitch up Beauty
the rusty bay
one white sock
(Grandpa said she was mine
and I said Wow
but we both knew that was dumb)
one black mane;
strapping her up
rigging her gear
(I couldn't even reach it all);
but we'd get everything to fit and feel right
and hitch onto the stone boat
and Go! Prancing
where the skids skimmed the snow
we'd be there by the reins
and old Beauty'd prance and fart
I always thought it smelled fantastic.

1963: Close Dancing

Around the age of 13, I was itching to get to second base with the girls. I did have some luck, but it was hard to come by and harder to sustain. This was the time of Saturday night parties, usually in some girl's basement with snacks provided by her parents who were under strict instructions to stay upstairs.

In preparation for these events, sometimes I'd grab a coffee can my mother was saving and get into my dad's liquor cabinet. I'd take a little bit out of five or six different bottles. Didn't matter what it tasted like, what mattered was not getting caught. Then I'd call a buddy or two and we'd meet out in the trees somewhere and drink this vile brew by passing the coffee can around till it was gone. More than once this resulted in puking before we got to the party. . . but that didn't mean you wouldn't get kissed. I sure owe a lot to all those good folks who made slow songs. Thank you.

Turns out that if you have to, you can slow dance to "The Duke of Earl."

1964: Mobility

By the time I was 15 I had graduated from a Moped (on which I could elude the cops in Junior High) to a Honda 50. The "50" means number of cubic centimeters displaced in the piston. It also means roughly the top speed. But if you laid out flat on it in a tail wind, you could get to 55. But my friend (who also had one) and I found a way to get to 70 mph.

I'd wrap old belts, ropes, chains, anything around the rear tire for traction so I could drive it all winter long in the snow and ice. But when the summer came the dangerous fun began. We figured out that if we'd get up behind a semi as it was leaving town at a lower speed, we could hang in there in the back draft created as it gained speed.

This way we'd find ourselves side by side on our little mo-torbikes going 70 mph down the highway three or four feet behind the back of these huge trucks.

Sometimes the draft would be a little erratic, swooshy, and make you wobble. When we were thinking clearly we'd then back off our throttles (which had to be at full bore for this drafting to work) and slowly fall back getting tossed around by the wind currents behind the truck.

I don't know for sure, but I think it was a dangerous means of reaching out to get separated from the world I was growing up in, which I called "terminal stability." It was time to move on.

1966: An Important Affirmation

My maternal grandmother, Mabel Dvorak, divorced my grandpa long before I was born and moved to town. Her father, my great grandfather, August Anderson, moved in with her. He was an old man when I was born, but lived to 102 and died when I was 18. Remarkably, and significantly to me, during his younger years he had made three trips by sea back to his native Sweden from the poor crude farming life in North Dakota. I still don't know how he did it.

When I was growing up he had a big gray mustache, wore vests, smoked a pipe, had a kind and gentle man-ner, and spent his afternoons on the back porch under the shade of the giant cottonwood trees. He'd sit there for hours with a tray on his lap and a bag of peanuts or stale bread. Squirrels and chipmunks and birds would come on to that tray and eat out of his hand. Rabbits would eat at his feet. He had a good collection of National Geographic and cuckoo clocks up in his room. He'd walk downtown into his 90's till he was hit by a car. He lived with his daughter till he had to go to the old folks home at around age 100, which was where he was when I needed him.

When I got back from my first trip to Europe and

North Africa, I was 17 and had just missed the first semester of my senior year. I also had long hair and a skeptical attitude toward American values and policies. After seven months on the road, my father refused to allow me back in the house because I refused to cut my hair. My mother cried every day until I couldn't bear it and cut it and moved home to give her peace in her heart. You can imagine my relations with my dad. I argued with my relatives about America's soul; I dressed out of the ordinary. I wore the same pair of blue jeans and flannel shirt every day for my senior year semester, but always kept them clean. I'd put away my childish things. You get the picture.

Needless to say I was alienated through actions of my own and the narrow-mindedness of family and friends. I had the strength of my convictions having had my mind and eyes opened on the roads of the world, but I was only 17, returning to a world that didn't understand me in North Dakota, and there was nothing there for reassurance, to say nothing of encouragement.

That is, there was nothing until my Grandma took me to see Great Grandpa August in the nursing home. As we walked into his room my Grandma said, "Dad, James is back from his long trip to Europe." Grandpa August looked up at me with a twinkle in his eye, a big smile opened on his face, he reached out both hands and clasped mine and looking me in the eye said, "You done fine boy."

It is the single most important sentence anyone ever spoke to me.

Grandfather's hands
were wide and strong
I'm happy
just to be them.

Interview

This is an edited version of an interview conducted in 2010. My friend Nora Antoine (Lakota) asked if I would be the subject of a study she was doing toward a PhD through Antioch College. The focus of the study was on the less explored dynamics of Cross-Cultural Activism.

What initially led you to become aware of Native American people and their struggle for their rights?
I grew up in Grand Forks, North Dakota. Geographically right between the Lakota and the Ojibway. Besides being a regional shopping center, Grand Forks is also a university town so for those reasons there were Native people in my periphery as a kid. And I remember being intrigued by the culture as we'd drive through a reservation on the way to a fishing lake. Upon entering one reservation in particular there was a sign that said, "You Are Now Leaving the State of Minnesota."

To the extent there was any mention of Indians among the grown-ups it was almost always in the perjorative. Strange as it may seem I should confess that I gained some of my interest and respect for Native culture by watching cowboy movies in the '50's. Although often portrayed as the bad guys, I saw past that characterization and felt a certain empathy for their plight, as well as admiration for what I perceived to be their wizened connection to the natural world – a more simple yet more colorful life than I had.

As I got up into my mid-teens my thoughts and perception deepened. I was restless and mistrusting of the lily white safe and suburban life I was surrounded by. I didn't think I was getting the whole picture of a life's possibilities; seemed like terminal stability to me (terminal to soul). So at 16 I took off traveling to Europe and North Africa. My eyes were opened by other cultures, particularly so-called "Third World" cultures and, by the end of my teenage years, I had back packed on four continents. I got a different look at the Judeo/Christian world views. They struck me as unnecessarily stark. Black and white and right and wrong seemed harshly and arbitrarily defined.

I saw that nature was not that way. I saw that indigenous cultures were not that way. I saw life as more cyclical and less linear. I studied and kept my eyes open and figured out that nature thrives in diversity. I thought about and studied monocultures, such as a climax forest that has become just pine trees. That made the forest very vulnerable to disease, and who can live in a monoculture of pine? Just the red squirrels. So it wasn't just susceptible to disease, it was boring too. I saw this as not just a metaphor for the Great White Way, but as a real world expression of these natural principles.

Therefore, I had a strong foundation of respect for indigenous people and their rights. Respecting diversity wasn't just good for minorities; it was good for all of us. I was sort of anti-authority by nature anyway so this seemed a natural evolution of thinking. Over time I travelled more around the world, worked when I had to and by the time I was 28 I had a Master's Degree in World Religions. This also gave me perspective on various world views and why people behave as they do.

After another year in the mostly rural parts of Asia, I landed in law school where I was drawn to the clinical program in the basement where students provided legal help to low-income people. I became the Student President of the clinic. My parents had raised me with the discipline for work. But I'd never really fancied it and only worked when I had to, never for more than a year at a time. It seemed to me that work takes so much of one's time (most of the daylight hours of life) that it better give you something more than just money. This thinking became extra significant as I was graduating from law school because I now had a wife, a son and a bunch of school loans. Days of intermittent work were behind me. It was career time.

I applied to a variety of nonprofit outfits, but the one that connected was running a little Indian legal aid office in Nebraska. So right out of law school I had a little office on a reservation. I had a partner doing farm law, but no secretary and no other Indian law attorneys around. We rented a small place on the rez and (this was 1984) I got paid $15,000 per year plus an extra $600 per year initially for "remote duty."

After I set up my desk and put some books on a shelf, I went to see each of the three tribes that had reservations in Nebraska. I worked with all three of them while living there for seven years, but the Winnebagos in particular really knew how to put me to work. It's now a quarter of a century later and I'm still doing Indian rights work through a nonprofit legal aid office.

What initial challenges did you encounter?

Although I was respectful of Native cultures in the abstract, I was quite naïve as to the specifics. This manifested as being inconsiderate without any bad intentions. Here's an embarrassing example: In my youth I had learned a descriptive phrase for how cold it is – "colder than a turd in a dead Eskimo." But the first time I used that phrase on the reservation the Indian guy I was with cocked his head and, saying nothing, looked at me very quizzically. Only then did it occur to me. Thereafter I changed "Eskimo" to "Polar Bear," but even then I may have offended some Bear clan people.

One initial challenge was trust. I didn't have a problem trusting the tribes and, when it comes to individuals, it's one person at a time, I don't care what color you are.

But tribal folks understandably had some hesitancy about trusting me. I totally get that. Not only did I arrive from a culture with a history of duplicity, exploitation and worse, but there's also this kind of creepy phenomenon of patronizing "do-gooders" who show up from time to time.

Sometimes the do-gooders have their own agenda of religious proselytizing or social activism, which means they aren't really there to learn and contribute. Which means they aren't really there with respect. And sometimes, even though they do want to contribute, their own cultural biases are just too strong. These are the kind of folks who tell the tribe what they "should" do. I've always been sensitive to that as these folks come and go. Indian people are more kind and cordial toward that than I think I would be, but anyway, fortunately, the do-gooder phenomenon is somehow sort of self-pruning.

Another challenge, for me at least, is a natural impulse to act quickly. In Indian Country decisions are often more deliberative. I saw that different pace bear fruit, and learned from it. But mostly the challenges I initially faced in relating to tribal people can be measured with humor. When they started teasing me it was an indication they welcomed me, liked me. When I started teasing back it was an indication to them that I was genuine. It was a strong indication we were in sync. Humor is a good indicator of trust, and it helps keep your spirit above some of the sorrow on the ground.

Who were significant people (either Native Americans or not) who supported your involvement with Native rights issues?

When I became an Indian rights attorney there were five individuals who made it clear to me that I was in the right place at the right time and doing the right work.

Reuben Snake comes first to mind. As Chairman of the Winnebago Tribe of Nebraska (and former national leader of the American Indian movement) he became my guide into the world of Indian rights. He started as a mentor and a client, which was a great, although unusual, combination. He became my friend – a word with deep and profound meaning to Winnebagos. He adopted me (along with numerous other non-Indians) as his brother. Eventually he became my best friend in the whole wide world. No pretense, no caution, no taboo subjects. I've never had a better friend. Never had a more important mentor. Worldly and wise and funny as hell.

Speaking of funny, the man with the quickest, wittiest and most profound sense of humor I've even known is Louie LaRose (Winnebago). By pedigree, I grew up serious and stoic in "suburban North Dakota" (not an oxymoron!). I learned a lot about relaxing those characteristics from traveling around the world. But it was Native America that really taught me about humor, allowed that part of my nature to open up. And no one was more instrumental in that than Louie. Now humor is a vital part of my personal and professional life – very important and very useful and, of course, a lot of fun. I wouldn't be where I am today with my wife, my kids or my profession without it. And I owe it all to Native America ... especially Louie and Reuben.

Then there's Bob Peregoy (Flathead), Walter Echo-Hawk (Pawnee) and Steve Moore (white mutt like me). Three great friends with whom I've co-counseled the best and biggest cases and projects of my career. While my work has been done through local, nonprofit Indian law offices, those guys were with the Native American Rights Fund, the most powerful and prestigious Indian rights law firm in the country. I'm deeply indebted to these skilful lawyers. Deeply grateful for their friendship with me and my family. The most enormous challenges of my career were all successfully accomplished and with style due to co-counseling with one or more of these guys.

How has your leadership evolved over time in working with Native activist people and organizations?

It has been very helpful to have always worked through a nonprofit law firm. That way none of my work or decision-making is colored by money. In over 25 years of Indian rights lawyering, I've never charged a client a dime. How many can say that?

Having always been the "Director" of a small office has freed me up to do what I want. Since there's way more to do than I have the budget to fund, it's been my philosophy to focus on work that has a broad and lasting impact for tribes. That might be protecting traditional Native religions or it might mean helping to develop tribal courts.

My leadership is secondary to the leadership of my clients. That's the main thing. After that, yes, I find I do get entrusted with decision-making, planning and even policy development. I understand Native thinking well enough to be comfortable with that honor and responsibility but only under two conditions: the first is that I am given those responsibilities by respected Native leaders, and the second is that there is always consultation and guidance from Native leaders. This work is not about me.

What have you learned about communication (written, verbal and nonverbal) in your work with Native rights people and groups?

I've learned to keep it real. It can be nuanced and sophisticated if my Native clients and colleagues like to think and talk that way. Or it can be straight forward and from the heart if they are inclined that way – which by the way is more common. Either way, the main thing is to keep it real. Be honest to the point of humility. And humor almost always furthers and enriches communication.

To the extent that appearances are a form of communication, working with Native people has been a real natural fit for me. I've always felt I was more readily accepted and trusted by Native people if I wasn't too dressed up. In the world I came from the fancier one was dressed the more respect and deference was accorded. You can't get away with such a shallow standard in Indian Country.

Reflecting back from your early experiences until now, what ideas or preconceived notions did you have that proved either true or false?

The only stereotype about Indian people that I've found true is that they always seem to have a lousy PA system. And even that one is less true now than it was 15 years ago.

Having travelled in the so-called Third World quite a bit before I got involved with Native Americans, I had a fair sense of the "intuitive, cyclical" thinking of indigenous people as opposed to the "rational, linear" thinking of "modern western" people. Some of the qualities of intuitive, cyclical thinking that I admire and have benefits from include: more respect for the natural world; less judgmental of others; more patience; and a healthy skepticism of rational, linear thinkers!

It hasn't been a shocking education to me... more a deepening, into my bones, of what I expected to find. But I am continually surprised (sometimes angered or embarrassed) at all the ill-informed and misinformed viewpoints of white America toward Native people. The level of ignorance can be truly astounding. And it does not seem to be directly related to levels of school education. If our modern systems collapsed I'd much rather be among Native people than in the great white world. I think it would be safer. Native people are more resilient and less likely to freak out.

How did you earn the trust of those you worked with and how did you come to trust those you affiliated within the Native rights community?

Mutual trust grows out of mutual respect. I have a

deep and profound respect for intuitive, cyclical thinking people, and I also have great respect for Native people's survivability in spite of all the hardship and racism that has gone on. Moreover, my sense of justice leads me toward their camp. I think my Native colleagues and clients perceive all that in me and that leads to their trust of me.

I've earned trust in part by being successful for my clients. I've been fortunate in that I've believed in my heart in all the large issues I've pursued with and for Native America. No doubt that has shown in my tenacity and level of commitment to the work. Living and working with Native people on a daily basis on a reservation for the first seven years of my career was a hugely positive aspect of mutually evolving trust.

What role did your close family members have in your decision to choose to work with Native rights and Native people?

I married well. Not that she had any money, but that she has a warm heart and an open mind. My wife too has an innate respect for other cultures, particularly indigenous ones. And she believes in the Buddhist notion of Right Livelihood: doing things that benefit others, that bring justice, that aren't selfish, that generate good karma. So she has been fully, naturally and generously supportive of what I do, even when it's meant being on the road a lot, and even though it's been at some financial sacrifice.

And it's much the same with our kids. Both of them have respected the work I do, and both have a good comfort level when moving around in other cultures. Much of the credit for the appreciation my family has for the work I do goes to Reuben Snake and Louie LaRose. They put a face on it for my family. I'm always so proud of the fact that my kids knew the great Reuben Snake as "Uncle Reuben."

And my great colleagues, perhaps especially the long

years with Bob, Walter and Steve, have given my family a strong sense of the dignity that goes with this work – to say nothing of the humor.

As for my extended family – not so much. My mother was proud of me because the work had heart and I was successful at it, but my father regrettably remained philosophically and politically predisposed against what I do right up to the end.

What do you consider your primary tangible or intangible successes or failures in working with Native rights and Native issues?

My legal career has been exclusively in Indian Law for more than 25 years. Not many lawyers, not many non-Indians, have the opportunity to participate in the evolution of Indian rights. I feel very fortunate. Professionally my successes have tended to be in the area of protecting traditional or spiritual values, and in developing tribal justice systems. These are two great areas near to my heart so it's like a blessing to have had the opportunity to focus my professional energy and skill in those areas.

I'm particularly proud of being appointed by the Winnebago Tribe to sit as a Justice in their Supreme Court for now into my second decade. I feel the responsibility and the honor.

On the personal side, well it isn't really a separate side. It's been an honor to be involved. It's given me "right livelihood" in a way that has nourished my soul and made my family proud. There haven't really been any failures. I'd just say that some successes haven't yet been fully accomplished.

What advice would you give to other Caucasian people interested in working with and/or promoting Native rights and interests?

I'd say if you're going to get into it just because it happens to be an available job, don't do it. This work involves the heart. If your heart isn't in tune with Native culture you likely won't find a harmonious life's work there. This work involves a respect for the spiritual. If you don't have a genuine respect for that you're likely to feel out of your element in this work.

If you come to this work with an unexamined "do-gooder" attitude about helping the poor Indians, it ain't gonna happen. You won't last. Indian people have seen that all before – by now, so have I. They're way past that. If you want to convert them to Christianity or modernity, stay away. Go convert your own people. If you think you're going to become Indian by osmosis or immersion, you're wrong and you'll be disappointed.

But if you have your own foundation and are comfortable with who you are; if you truly believe in social justice; if you insist that your work give you something besides money; if you want to advance the interests of Native people according to their terms – well, then you might make it. And if you do, you're among the fortunate because there's not much better work out there. Very rewarding in unexpected ways.